The Guillet Family Tree

Ramona Davidson

*Our mission is to efficiently provide the world's finest, most comprehensive book publishing
service, enabling every author to experience success. To find out how to publish your book,
your way, and have it available worldwide, visit us online at www.trafford.com*

Trafford rev. 10/11/2010

 www.trafford.com

North America & international
toll-free: 1 888 232 4444 (USA & Canada)
phone: 250 383 6864 ♦ fax: 812 355 4082

The Guillet Family Tree was compiled through family records, letters, family statements, interviews, and many years of research, along with a collection of photos and documents. My hope is to educate future generations by helping them understand where their family root started.

Thank you to all who have contributed in the making of this book. Special thanks to my husband Brian, daughters Tanya and Jamie, and my mother Annette for their patience with me while I completed my dream.
-Ramona

Ramona Davidson
P.O. Box 1212
Chetwynd, BC, Canada V0C 1J0
250-788-3436
Email: brdavidson@persona.ca

5

This book is dedicated to my family,
along with the dream that their memories
will live on through these pages.
Generations have come and gone,
Some I will never know except for the fragile photos
and maybe a forgotton letter, now yellow with age,
left in a corner of the attic.

While compiling their stories and photos,
I was caught up into the lives of our ancestory.
I wish I could step back in time to meet the ones of whom we come from.
To share their secrets, their joys and be part of their stories.
Then it would be easy to fill in between the lines.

But for now I will continue to gather my family's history
onto these pages with the pictures of the past
and stories from the ones that were part of those forgotten memories.

I am only part of the tree and a piece of me is tucked into each page.
For these memories are a part of who I am
to be passed onto my children and to theirs.
Author Unknown

Ramona (Nee Guillet) Davidson

Francois Guillet
and
Marie (Nee Pluchon) Guillet

GENERATION 1

1.   Francois Guillet-1[1] was born on 02 Jan 1854 in Venee, France. He died in 1932 in Domremy, Saskatchewan. He married Marie Pluchon. She was born on 31 Mar 1857. She died on 15 Nov 1920 in Domremy, Saskatchewan.

Notes for Francois Guillet:
Francois Guillet boarded a boat destined for Canada. With him were his wife Marie (Pluchon) and their seven children: Francois, Arthe, Aristide, Clement, Alexis, Henri and one-year-old Eugene. From the point of docking, the family traveled on the train until they reached Duck Lake, Saskatchewan. The family moved to Domremy and made their home on a newly purchased homestead east of the original site of the town of Domremy. Francois Guillet was one of the first settlers of the old Domremy settlement, sometimes referred to as the "old mission". It was in 1895 that the inhabitants from this mission decided to call the small hamlet Domremy, named after the birthplace of their patron saint, St. Joan of Arc, in France.

Francois lost two sons after arrival. In 1896 Francois died at the age of 16 from pneumonia he caught while digging a well. A younger son, Clement, died at the age of seven in 1897. Both sons are buried in the old cemetery. However two more children were born in Canada: Louise in 1897 and Camille in 1900.

School records indicate that Eugene, Henri and Louise started school in January, 1904 at the first temporary school held in Father Barbier's house. The teacher was Sister St. Sylvester, the first teacher to teach in the area. In January 1905, the first school was built with logs and a class of 25-30 students moved in. In 1907 Camille started school in the new building.

Francois raised his family on his homestead. His children were naturally musical like their father who played the violin by ear. All the boys learned to play the violin and this musical talent was passed on to many of Francois' descendants.

On November 15, 1920, at age 63, Marie passed away and was buried in the old cemetery. Francois moved to town and lived in a building next to Clement Guillet. When Francois realized that he couldn't be buried in the old cemetery, he had his sons Louis, Eugene, Henri and Alexis move his wife and two sons to the new cemetery. In 1932 Francois passed away at his son, Alexis' home.

The original home that Francois built was still standing in 1995. Louis and his family resided in the home until 1941, then Camille and her husband Alex Either lived in it for a short time in 1941. The home was sold to Carl Kusch and in 1975 sold to the present owner Jean Denis and family.

Louis, Alexis, Eugene and Camille

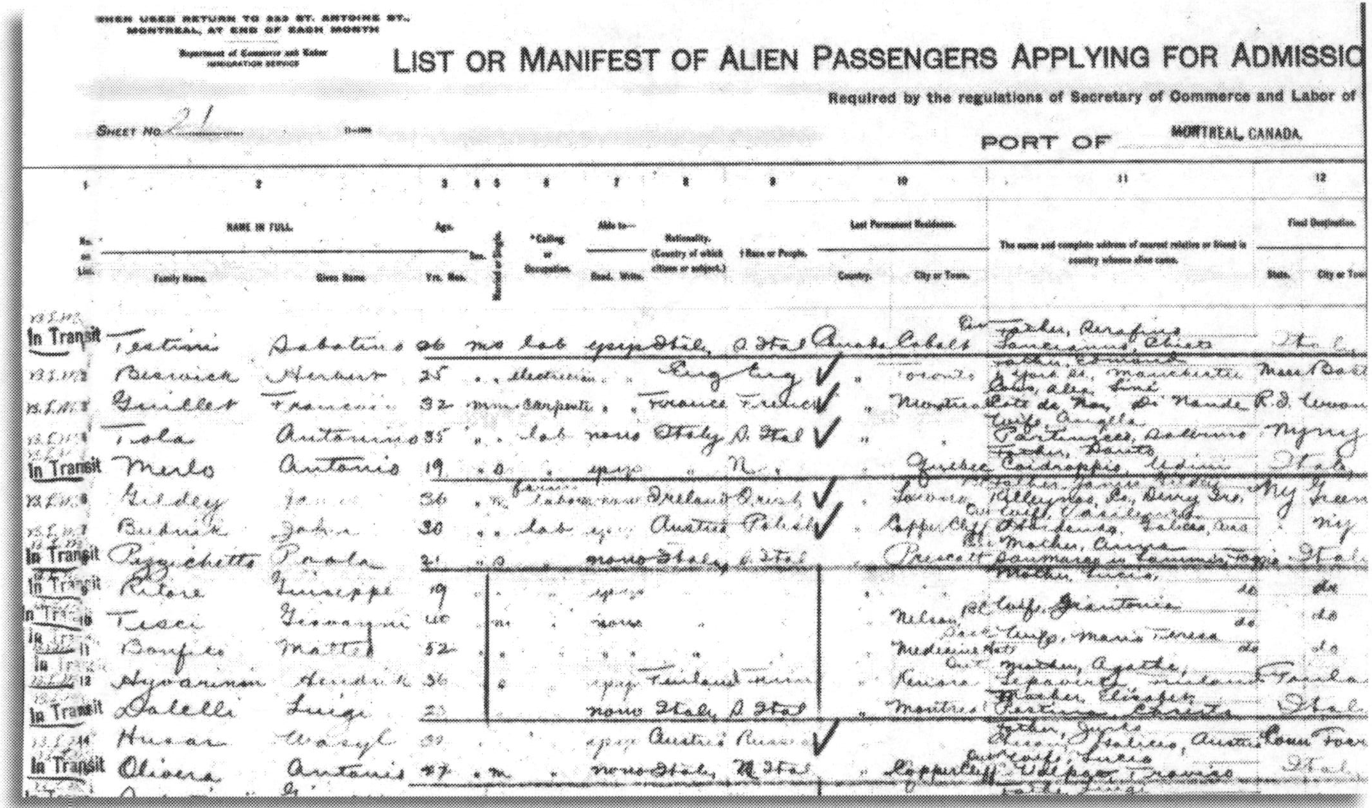

WHEN USED RETURN TO 283 ST. ANTOINE ST., MONTREAL, AT END OF EACH MONTH

Department of Commerce and Labor
Immigration Service

LIST OR MANIFEST OF ALIEN PASSENGERS APPLYING FOR ADMISSIO

Required by the regulations of Secretary of Commerce and Labor of

Sheet No. 21

PORT OF MONTREAL, CANADA.

Status	Family Name	Given Name	Age	Calling or Occupation	Nationality	Race or People	Last Permanent Residence (City or Town)
In Transit	Testini	Sabatino	26	lab	Italy	S. Ital	Cobalt
	Beswick	Herbert	25	electrician	Eng	Eng	Toronto
	Gaillet	Francois	32	carpenter	France	French	Montreal
	Tola	Antonino	35	lab	Italy	S. Ital	
In Transit	Merlo	Antonio	19			N.	Quebec
	Gildey	James	36	labourer	Ireland	Irish	
	Budnik	John	30	lab	Austria	Polish	Copper Cliff
In Transit	Pizzichetto	Paola	21		Italy	S. Ital	Prescott
In Transit	Ritore	Giuseppe	19				
In Transit	Tesci	Giovanni	40				Nelson
In Transit	Bonfico	Matteo	52				Medicine Hat
In Transit	Hyvarinen	Hendrik	36		Finland	Finn	Kenora
In Transit	Dalelli	Luigi	23		Italy	S. Ital	Montreal
	Husar	Wasyl	[illegible]		Austria	Russ	
In Transit	Olivera	Antonio	47		Italy	N. Ital	Copper Cliff

Children of Francois Guillet and Marie Pluchon are:

2.   i.   Alexis Guillet, B: France, D: 1953 in Domremy, SK, M: Jan. 1909 in Domremy, SK.

    ii.   Francois Guillet, B: 1880, D: 1896 in Domremy, SK at age 16.

3.   iii. Aristide Guillet, B: 1883 in France, D: 1938, M: 18 Feb 1918 in Domremy, SK.

4.   iv. Marthe Guillet, B: 07 Sep 1884 in Vendee, France, D: 26 Nov 1969 in Edmonton, AB, M: 1903 in Domremy, SK.

5.   v.   Henri Francois Guillet, B: 11 Sep 1889 in La Boursier, France, D: 08 May 1974 in Domremy, SK, M:19 Aug 1914 in St. Joan of Arc Catholic Church Domremy, SK.

6.   vi   Clement Guillet, B: 1890, D: 1897 in France at age 7.

7.   vii. Eugene Leon Guillet, B: 23 May 1894 in La Boissarre, France, D: 05 May 1966 in Prince Albert, SK, M: 23 Sep 1920 in Batoche, SK.

8.   viii. Louis Guillet, B: 12 Mar 1898 in Domremy, SK, D: 14 Feb 1964 in Prince Albert, SK, 11 Jan 1920 in Domremy, SK.

9.   ix. Camille Guillet, B: 15 Aug 1900, D: 07 Apr 1980, M: 09 May 1927 in Prince Albert, SK.

Grandpa Francois and son Alexis

GENERATION 2

2. Alexis Guillet-2 (Francois Guillet-1) was born in France. He died in 1953 in Domremy, SK. He married Georgina Chartier in Jan 1909 in Domremy SK, daughter of Napoleon Chartier and Helene. She died in 1945 at Domremy, SK. Alexis built a store at the mission, the original site of Domremy.

Children of Alexis Guillet and Georgina Chartier are:
   i. Helen Guillet, B: 1914, M: 1937.
   ii. Denise Guillet, B: 1925.
   iii. Florence Guillet, B: 1928.
   iv. Walter Guillet, B: 1912 in Domremy, SK, D: Schreiber, ON, M: 1936.

Walter, Helen and Alexis

3. Aristide Guillet-2(Francois Guillet-1 was born in 1883 in France. He died in Domremy, SK in 1938. He married Maria Lequalt on 18 Feb 1918 in Domremy, SK. She was born on 12 Apr 1896 in France. She died in Nov 1958 in Prince Albert, SK.

Children of Aristide Guillet and Maria Lequalt are:
   i. Edmond Guillet, B: 27 Nov 1919 in Domremy, SK, D: 25 Jan 1990 in Domremy, SK.
10. ii. Yvonne Guillet was adopted in 1936.

Maria (nee Lequalt) and Aristide Guillet

Aristide, Maria and son Edmond

15

4. Marthe Guillet-2 (Francois Guillet-1) was born on 07 Sept 1884 in Vendee, France. She died on 26 Nov 1969 in Edmonton, AB. She married Bruno Baribeau in 1903 in Domremy, SK. Bruno was born on 12 Mar 1883. He died on 21 Mar 1952.

Children of Marthe Guillet and Bruno Baribeau are:

11. i.   Denise Baribeau, B: 1916, M: 08 Sep 1939.

Marthe and Bruno Baribeau

12. ii. Irene Baribeau, B: 1914, D: 1977.
13. iii. Laure Baribeau, B: 1915, D: 1989.
14. iv. George Baribeau, B: 1906 in Domremy, SK, D: 1970.
15. v.   Lucien Baribeau, B: 1905 in Prince Albert, SK.
16. vi. Alida Baribeau, B: 1907, D: 1981.
17. vii. Helene Baribeau, B: 1909.

5. Henri Francois Guillet-2 (Francois Guillet-1) was born on 11 Sept 1889 in La Boursier, France. He died on 08 May 1974 in Domremy, SK. He married Jeanne Marie Joubert on 19 Aug 1914 in St. Joan of Arc Catholic Church Domremy, SK, daughter of Auguste Louis Benjamin Joubert and Marie Louise Grolleau. She was born on 21 Jun 1896 in Marieul SurLay Vendee, France. She died on 17 Sept 1982 in Domremy, SK.

Henri and Jeanne Guillet

Children of Henri Francois Guillet and Jeanne Marie Joubert are:

18. i.   Edward Guillet, B: 20 Oct 1919 in Wakaw, SK, M: 13 Apr 1943 in Hudson Bay, SK.
19. ii. Clement Guillet, B: 21 Feb 1922 in Hoey, SK, D: 17 Mar 1986 in Wakaw, SK, M: 27 Aug 1945 in Kelowna, BC.

20.   iii.   Felix Guillet, B: 14 Jul 1927 in Domremy, SK, D: 25 Jan 2007 in Nipawin, SK, M: 03 Nov 1949 in Cudworth, SK.

21.   iv.   Henriette Guillet, B: 04 Jun 1915 in Domremy, SK, M: 14 Oct 1936 in Domremy, SK.

22.   v.   Alice Gabrielle Guillet, B: 18 May 1916 in Domremy, SK, M: 14 Oct 1936 in Domremy, SK.

23.   vi.   Lorraine Guillet, B: 29 Dec 1935 in Domremy, SK, M: 29 Oct 1953 in Jean Cote, AB.

24.   vii.   Gabrielle Guillet, B: 01 Apr 1918 in Wakaw, SK, D: 22 Jul 1980 in Prince Albert, SK, M: 06 Oct 1939 in Domremy, SK.

6.   Eugene Leon Guillet-2 (Francois Guillet-1) was born on 23 May 1894 in La-Boissarre, France. He died on 05 May 1966 in Prince Albert, SK. He married Angeline Georgine Pilon on 23 Sep 1920 in Saskatchewan, daughter of Joseph Pilon and Julienne Braconnier. She was born on 08 Dec 1900 in Batoche, SK. She died on 23 Sep 1997 in Regina, SK.

Eugene Guillet

Children of Eugene Leon Guillet and Angeline Georgine Pilon are:

25.   i.   Agnes Guillet, B: 22 Sep 1921 in Domremy, SK.

26.   ii.   Gilbert Guillet, B: 13 Nov 1922 in Domremy, SK, D: 20 Sep 2001 in Domremy, SK.

27.   iii.   Johnny Guillet, B: 08 Aug 1924 in Domremy, SK, D: 07 Jan 2000 in Regina, SK.

28.   iv.   Frances Guillet, B: 08 Jan 1926 in Domremy, SK, D: 07 Sep 2003 in Regina, SK, M: 21 Sep 1949 in Domremy, SK.

1920, September 20 - Angeline and Eugene Guillet Wedding

29.   v.   Irene Guillet, B: 12 May 1928 in Domremy, SK, M: 24 Nov 1949 in Domremy, SK.

30.   vi.   Leon Guillet, B: 08 May 1930 in Domremy, SK, D: 04 Dec 1999 in Kamloops, BC, M: 28 Jul 1949 in Regina, SK

31.   vii.   Aline Guillet, B: 26 Mar 1933 in Domremy, SK, M: 07 Apr 1953.

32.   viii. Raymond Albert Guillet, B: 06 Sep 1936 in Domremy, SK [2], M: 05 Jan 1957 in Vancouver, BC

ix.   Paul Ernest Guillet, B: 22 May 1951 in Regina, SK

1936 - Leon, Aline and Irene
(West Side of House in Domremy)

Angeline and Eugene Guillet

Agnes, Gilbert, Johnny (with tie), Frances

1920, September 20 - Angeline
and Eugene Guillet Wedding

Eugene Guillet

12 M. D. **1st** ....Depot Battalion........ **Sask.** ....Regiment

Regtl. No **3354886**

PARTICULARS OF RECRUIT Coy 6
DRAFTED UNDER MILITARY SERVICE ACT, 1917

(Class........**1**........)

1. Surname .... **Guillet**
2. Christian Name .... **Eugene**
3. Present Address .... **Domremy P.O. Sask.**
4. Military Service Act letter and number ... **420790**
5. Date of birth .... **May 23 1894**
6. Place of birth .... **Vandee Co., France**
   (town, township or county and country)
7. Married, widower or single .... **Single**
8. Religion .... **R Catholic**
9. Trade or calling .... **Farmer**
10. Name of next-of-kin .... **Francois Guillet**
11. Relationship of next-of-kin .... **Father**
12. Address of next-of-kin .... **Domremy P.O. Sask.**
13. Whether at present a member of the Active Militia **No**
14. Particulars of previous military or naval service, if any. **None**
15. Medical Examination under Military Service Act:

    (a) Place **Prince Albert Sask.** **Nov 7 1917** (c) Category **A 2**

*Eugene Guillet
in Army Attire*

DECLARATION OF RECRUIT

I, ...**Eugene Guillet**........, do solemnly declare that the
above particulars refer to me, and are true.

Eugene Guillet ....(Signature of Recruit)

DESCRIPTION ON CALLING UP

Apparent age .... **24** yrs. **1** mths.		Distinctive marks, and marks indicating congenital peculiarities or previous disease.
Height .... **5** ft. **6** ins.		
Chest measurement { fully expanded **34** ins.		
range of expansion **3** ins.		
Complexion .... **Dark**		
Eyes .... **Brown**		
Hair .... **Fair**		

.... O.C. ....Depot Btln.

........Regt.

Place ....**Regina Sask.**........ Date ....**July 10 1918**
M. F. W. 133.

20

7. Louis Guillet-2 (Francois Guillet-1) was born on 12 Mar 1898 in Domremy, SK. She died on 14 Feb 1964 in Prince Albert, SK. She married Rolande Joubert on 11 Jan 1920 in Domremy, SK, son of Auguste Louis Benjamin Joubert and Marie Louise Grolleau. He was born on 24 Aug 1901 in Domremy, SK. He died on 17 Jun 1988 in Prince Albert, SK.

Children of Louis Guillet and Rolande Joubert are:

33.   i.   Marcel Guillet, B: 31 Oct 1922 in Domremy, SK, D: 14 Oct 1971 in Prince Albert, SK.

Louis (Back) Roland Joubert (front) Camille (front) with her hsuband

34.   ii.   Elise Marie Rollande Guillet, B: 21 Sep 1923 in Wakaw, SK, M: 23 Sep 1946 in Prince Albert, SK.

8. Camille Guillet 2 (Francois Guillet-1) was born on 15 Aug 1900. She died on 07 Apr 1980. She married Alex Ethier on 09 May 1927 in Prince Albert, SK. He was born on 30 Jun 1902 in Crookston, Minnesota. He died on 10 Apr 1991.

Camille Guillet

Children of Camille Guillet and Alex Ethier are:

35. i. Laura Ethier, M: 01 Mar 1954.
    ii. Georgeine Ethier, M: Mar 1952 in Domremy, SK.
    iii. Eugene Ethier, B: 23 Nov 1928, M: 12 Jul 1954.
36. iv. Andre Ethier, B: 04 Nov 1930, D: 02 Jun 1981, M: 1956 in Canora.
    v. Norman Ethier, B: 04 Apr 1936, M: 13 Jul 1962.
37. vi. Clarence Ethier, B: 18 Apr 1941, M: 04 Nov 1963 in Prince Albert, SK.
38. vii. Daniel Ethier, B: 11 Mar 1945.

GENERATION 3

9. Walter Guillet-3 (Alexis Guillet-2, Francois Guillet-1) was born in 1912 in Domremy, SK. He died in Schreiber, Ontario. He married Marie Louise Roy in 1936. She died in Schreiber, ON.

GUILLET, Marie "Louise" (Grama "G") Monday, April 2, 2007. Mrs. Marie "Louise" Guillet (Grama "G"), age 90 years resident of Schreiber, Ontario passed away peacefully in Thunder Bay Regional Health

Walter and Marie Guillet

Sciences Centre on Thursday, April 27, 2006. Mom was born in Vonda, Saskatchewan and moved to Domremy, Saskatchewan where she resided with her late husband Walter Guillet and four children until 1943 at which time they moved to Schreiber with CP Rail. There, mom had five more children. Mom was a very loving and giving woman. Mom's greatest joy in life was her devotion to loving and raising her family. She was a very compassionate mother and grandmother who gave endlessly to the raising of her nine children and many grandchildren. For over thirty years, after the passing of Walter, mom was the sole provider of her family. Mom's inner strength came from her religious belief that whatever she truly needed God would provide. She worked many years as a cook and waitress at Birch Motors Restaurant and also as a custodian for Bell Canada never complaining. The welcome mat was always out for anyone and everyone. Mom will be missed greatly for her love, support and her delightful sense of humor. Mom was a long time active member of the Catholic Women's League. Mom is survived by her 6 children Robert, Raymond (Margaret), Lawrence (DeNeille), Dennis, Darlene Porier (Paul), Jocelyn Reynolds (Doug), son-in-law Gerry Thrower and many grandchildren, great-grandchildren, nieces and nephews. Mom was predeceased by her husband Walter, her parents Florida and Hudor Roy and her children Diane, Evelyn Thrower and Suzanne Beaucage (Ernie), and daughter-in-law Evelyn Guillet. Funeral services for the late Mrs. Marie "Louise" Guillet will be held on Wednesday,

May 3, 2006 at 11:00 AM with family and friends gathering at Holy Angels Roman Catholic Church in Schreiber for the Funeral Mass celebrated by Fr. Antoni Fujarczuk. Interment of Ashes to follow in the Schreiber Cemetery. If friends so desire, donations can be made to McCausland Hospital Long Term Care. Arrangements entrusted to the EVEREST FUNERAL CHAPEL, 299 Waverley St. at Algoma.

Children of Walter Guillet and Marie Louise Roy are:
  i.   Suzanne Guillet.
  ii.   Evelyne Guillet.

Notes for Evelyne Guillet:
THROWER, Evelyn November 12, 2004-Mrs. Evelyn Thrower beloved wife of Gerald (Gerry) Thrower of Schreiber Ontario passed away peacefully on November 10, 2004. Evelyn was born in Saskatchewan and moved to Schreiber, Ontario where she met and married Gerry Thrower. She was very family oriented and enjoyed her grandchildren immensely. She always ensured her family knew they were loved and she always had a hug for them. Even through her illness Evelyn always managed to have smile when they came to visit her in hospital. Evelyn was a very supportive, caring and understanding woman. She believed material things were not so important. She loved working at the restaurants for many years and will be remembered by young and old. She was a very proud, intelligent and extremely innovative woman. Herquiet, pleasant personality was atremendous influence on her children. A few of her nicknames at home were Froggy, Sa-pee-toots, Ma and Kermit. Evelyn was very well known for enjoying Halloween and making costumes with one of her closest friends (Annette). Evelyn will be sadly missed by her husband Gerry, children Carrie-Jane, Craig, Karen (Roy) and Michael (Cindy), grandchildren Matthew, Kevin, Brittany, Jerry and Drew, mother Louise Guillet, sisters Jocelyn, Darlene, Suzanne and brothers Dennis, Robert, Lawrence and Raymond. Evelyn was predeceased by her father Walter and sister Diane and in-laws William Thrower (Bill) and mother-in-law Nettie-Jane. Mom was nothing short of an amazing woman that taught us what is truly important in life. She will be remembered and cherished in our hearts and loved always.

A memorial will be held for Evelyn at the Schreiber Legion hall on Saturday, November 13, 2004, beginning at 11:00 a.m. As expressions of sympathy, donations to the McCausland Hospital Long Term Care Project or Northern Cancer Research would be appreciated.

iii. Robert Guillet, B: 20 Mar 1939, D: 27 Nov 2007.

Notes for Robert Guillet:
Wednesday, December 5, 2007
Robert Walter Guillet was born on March 20th, 1939 in Domremy, Saskatchewan. On November 27th, 2007, Robert passed peacefully into the Arms of Our Lord with his wife Yvonne by his side that lovingly cared for him during his illness.

Robert received his Quarter Century Club Award from Canadian Motorways Ltd. In 1992, as well as driving transport trucks and was shop steward until retirement in 1993. Robert was also a member of the Prairie Teamsters Union and served on it sexecutive board. Robert also worked with the Injured Workers Support Group Of Thunder Bay & District, as a volunteer, passed president, vice-president, andtreasurer active members who generally enhanced the Injured Workers Support Group. Robert was predeceased by his son Robbie in 1983 and his first wife Eveline in 1998, by his parents Walter and Louise Guillet, also sisters Evelyn Thrower of Schreiber and Suzanne Beaucage of Thunder Bay.Robert is survived by his second wife Yvonne, daughter Janette Stoot (Fred) and grandchildren Daniel, Steven and Jennifer Stoot; all of Colorado Springs, Colorado USA and stepson Brett Dowton, brothers Raymond (Margaret) of Windsor, Lawrence (DeNeille) of Atikokan, Dennis of Thunder Bay, sisters Darlene Guillet (Paul) Toronto, Jocelyn Reynolds (Doug) of Schreiber. Robert is also survived byseveral aunts and uncles and cousins in Saskatchewan plus nieces andnephews in Thunder Bay and Schreiber. AlsoRobert's first wife s daughter Linda Wragg (Brian), Linda's daughter Crystal Hull (Ian) Crystal's daughter Taylor Hull. Acremation has taken place with a privateinterment in keeping with Robert s wishes. A very special thank you to the staff of CCAC especially Lorraine, the V.O.N. nurses Katherine, Melisa, Judy, Roxanne and any I may have missed. Support-care workers Ryan and Paul, thank you for all the help and guidance.

GUILLET, Robert Walter Tuesday, December 4, 2007
It is with great sorrow that the family of Mr. Robert Walter Guillet announces his passing on November 27, 2007 at the age of 68. Robert was born on March 20, 1939 in Domremy, Sask. where he spent most of his early years. The family later moved to Schreiber, Ontario. Robert married Eveline Caissie in Thunder Bay on June 29, 1963 where they resided for many years. Robert worked driving trucks and retired from Motorways in the early 1990s. Robert believed strongly in helping his fellow workers through his involvement in the Thunder Bay District Injured WorkersSupport Gr any friends will lovingly remember Robert. Robert is survived by his daughter Linda Wragg (Brian) of Thunder Bay, his grand daughter Crystal Hull (Ian) his great grand daughter Taylor of Halifax, and two brothers Raymond Guillet (Margaret) of Windsor, brother Lawrence Guillet (DeNeille) of Atikokan, brother Dennis Guillet of Thunder Bay. He is also survived by his sisters Jocelyn Reynolds (Doug) of Schreiber and Darlene Poirier (Paul) of Etobicoke, as well as many nieces and nephews. Robert was predeceased by his wife Eveline in 1989, his son "Robbie" in 1983 and parents Walter and Louise Guillet of Schreiber, sister Evelyn Thrower of Schreiber and sister Suzanne Beaucage of Thunder Bay. Cremation has taken place and at Robert s request no funeral service will be held. If so desired, donations may be made to the Thunder Bay District Injured Workers Support Group (Rm. 17, Lakehead Labour Centre, 929 Fort William Road, Thunder Bay, Ont. P7B 3A6) or charity of your choice.

    iv. Raymond Guillet.
    v. Lauence Guillet.
    vi. Diane Guillet, D: died at a young age.
    vii. Dennis Guillet.
    viii. Darlene Guillet.
    ix. Jocelyn Guillet.

10. Yvonne Guillet-3 (Aristide Guillet-2, Francois Guillet-1).

    i. Marcel Guillet.
    ii. Norman Guillet.
    iii. Denis Guillet.
    iv. Denise Guillet.

11. Denise Baribeau-3 (Marthe Guillet-2, Francois Guillet-1) was born in 1916. She married Ernest Bastide on 08 Sep 1939.

Children of Denise Baribeau and Ernest Bastide are:
  i.   Maurice Bastide.
  ii. Louise Bastide.
  iii. Ernie Bastide.
  iv. Raymond Bastide.

12. Irene Baribeau-3 (Marthe Guillet-2, Francois Guillet-1) was born in 1914. She died in 1977. She married Mr. Villeneuve.

Child of Irene Baribeau and Mr. Villeneuve is:
  i.   Paulette Villeneuve.

13. Laure Baribeau-3 (Marthe Guillet-2, Francois Guillet-1) was born in 1915. She died in 1989. She married Mr. Blackstock.

Child of Laure Baribeau and Mr. Blackstock is:
  i.   Berna Blackstock.

14. George Baribeau-3 (Marthe Guillet-2, Francois Guillet-1) was born in 1906 in Domremy, SK. He died in 1970. He married Miss Juliette.

Children of George Baribeau and Juliette (Unknown) are:
  i.   Jacqueline Baribeau.
  ii. Lorraine Baribeau.
  iii. Yvonne Baribeau.
  iv. Beatrice Baribeau.

15. Lucien Baribeau-3 (Marthe Guillet-2, Francois Guillet-1) was born in 1905 in Prince Albert.

    i.   Raymond Baribeau.

16. Alida Baribeau-3 (Marthe Guillet-2, Francois Guillet-1) was born in 1907. She died in 1981. She married Mr. Stone.

    Child of Alida Baribeau and Mr. Stone is:
        i.   Loretta Baribeau.

17. Helene Baribeau-3 (Marthe Guillet-2, Francois Guillet-1) was born in 1909. She married Mr. Legault.

    Child of Helene Baribeau and Mr. Legault is:
        i.   Robert Legault.

18. Edward Guillet-3 (Henri Francois Guillet-2, Francois Guillet-1) was born on 20 Oct 1919 in Wakaw, SK. He married Mary Irene Ethier on 13 Apr 1943 in Hudson Bay, SK, daughter of Ernest Joseph Ethier and Ida Ella Prediger. She was born on 15 Sep 1924 in Carlton, SK at Grandmother's house.

Edward and Irene Guillet
50th Wedding Anniversary

Children of Edward Guillet and Mary Irene Ethier are:

38.   i.   Sharyn Edith Dianne Guillet, B: 14 Jun 1949 in Hudson Bay, SK, M: 26 Jul 1969 in Chetwynd, BC.

39.   ii. Dennis Edward Norman Guillet, B: 18 Jan 1944 in Hudson Bay, SK, M: 10 Aug 1968 in Chetwynd, BC.

40.   iii. Ernest Henry Guillet, B: 20 Sept 1945 in Hudson Bay, SK, M: 07 Nov 1964 in Chetwynd, BC.

41.   iv. Donald Lorne Guillet, B: 03 Dec 1946 in Hudson Bay, SK, M: 25 Feb 1967 in Chetwynd, BC.

42.   v.   Leslie Gordon Guillet, B: 08 Oct 1947 in Hudson Bay, SK.

43.   vi. Norman Daryl Guillet, B: 04 Jul 1955 in McLennan, AB, M: 08 Oct 1977 in Chetwynd, BC.

      vii. Debra Jeanette Guillet, B: 05 Dec 1956 in Manning, AB.

44.   viii. Sandra Lynn Guillet, B: 31 Jul 1958 in Dawson Creek, BC, M: 25 Jul 2003 in Dawson Creek, BC.

45.   ix. Janice Laurelle Guillet, B: 03 Jun 1960 in Dawson Creek, BC, M: 09 Oct 1982.

46.   x.   Edward Maurice Guillet Jr., B: 10 Oct 1961 in Dawson Creek, BC.

47.   xi. Kevin Joseph Guillet, B: 10 Apr 1965 in Dawson Creek, BC, M: 30 Mar 1985 in Chetwynd, BC.

19. Clement Guillet-3 (Henri Francois Guillet-2, Francois Guillet-1) was born on 21 Feb 1922 in Hoey, SK. He died on 17 Mar 1986 in Wakaw, SK. He married Marquerite Poitras on 27 Aug 1945 in Kelowna, BC. She was born on 01 Apr 1926 in Marcelin, SK.

Children of Clement Guillet and Marquerite Poitras are:

48.   i.   Dorina Guillet, B: 03 Sep 1946 in Cudworth, SK, M: 31 Aug 1968 in Domremy, SK.

Clement and Marguerite Guillet

49. ii. Gerald Guillet, B: 27 Jul 1949 in Cudworth, SK, M: 01 Sep 1973 in Birsay, SK.
50. iii. Lucille M. Guillet, B: 10 Feb 1951 in Cudworth, SK, M: 03 Jul 1976 in Domremy, SK.
51. iv. Robert Guillet, B: 17 May 1952 in Cudworth, SK, M: 03 Jul 1976 in a double wedding with Lucille and Michael.
52. v. Maurice Guillet, B: 24 Jun 1959 in Wakaw, SK, M: 06 Aug 1988.
53. vi. Mark Harold Guillet, B: 18 Nov 1963 in Wakaw, SK, M: 25 Apr 1992.

Clement Guillet Family: (Back) Warren, Terry, Renee, Bob, Etta, Janet, Mark, Joyce, Gerry, Lucille, Leanne, Mike. (Middle) Dorina, Michelle, Marguerite, Chantelle, Andrea, Maurice. (Front) Danielle, Lisa, Andre, Dean, Andrea

20. Felix Guillet-3 (Henri Francois Guillet-2, Francois Guillet-1) was born on 14 Jul 1927 in Domremy, SK. He died on 25 Jan 2007 in Nipawin, SK. He married Josephine Yuzik on 03 Nov 1949 in Cudworth, SK. She was born on 10 Mar 1931 in Cudworth, SK.

Children of Felix Guillet and Josephine Yuzik are:
54. i.   Daniel Guillet, B: 13 Mar 1950 in Domremy, SK, D: 22 Aug 2004, M: 12 May 1973 in Yellowknife, NWT.
     ii. Ronald Francis Guillet, B: 05 May 1952, M: 30 Apr 1990.
     iii. Richard Guillet, B: 25 Jul 1956 in Wakaw, SK, M: 21 May 1977 in Birch Hills, SK.
55. iv. Linda Guillet, B: 27 Jun 1958 in Domremy, SK, M: 18 Dec 1975 in Nipawin, SK.
     v.   Faye Maureena Guillet, B: 13 Apr 1970 in Nipawin, SK.

21. Henriette Guillet-3 (Henri Francois Guillet-2, Francois Guillet-1) was born on 04 Jun 1915 in Domremy, SK. She married Louise Ethier on 14 Oct 1936 in Domremy, SK. He was born on 17 May 1914 in Domremy, SK. He died on 16 Aug 2001 in Domremy, SK.

Children of Henriette Guillet and Louise Ethier are:
56. i.   Anita Marie Cecile Ethier, B: 19 Sep 1937 in Prince Albert, SK, M: 27 Oct 1953 in Marie Reine, AB.
57. ii. Edouard Charles Maurice Ethier, B: 06 Jan 1939 in St. Louis, SK, M: 31 May 1969 in Dawson Creek, BC.
58. iii. Denise Marie Ethier, B: 18 May 1944 in Prince Albert, SK, M: 28 Oct 1961 in Chetwynd, BC.
59. iv. Leo Ethier, B: 29 Jul 1945 in Prince Albert, SK, M: 14 Oct 1966 in Peace River, BC.
60. v.   Maurice Joseph Ethier, B: 21 Apr 1949 in Prince Albert, SK, M: 14 Jun 1975 in Chetwynd, BC.
61. vi. Aline Marie Ethier, B: 29 Jul 1951 in Peace River, BC, M 08 Aug 1970 in Chetwynd, BC.
62. vii Jean Ethier, B: 15 Jan 1940, D: 15 Jan 1940.

22. Alice Gabrielle Guillet-3 (Henri Francois Guillet-2, Francois Guillet-1) was born on 18 May 1916 in Domremy, SK. She married Robert Alderic Ethier on 14 Oct 1936 in Domremy, SK, son of Ernest Ethier and Ida Prediger. He was born on 30 Jun 1915. He died on 01 Sep 1963 in Sudbury, ON. She married Wilfred Lepage on 19 Aug 1978 in Levack, ON. He was born on 28 Jan 1920 in Hanmer, ON. He died on 23 Jan 2004 in Lively, ON.

Children of Alice Gabrielle Guillet and Robert Alderic Ethier are:
62.   i.   Leonard Ronald Ethier, B: 03 Oct 1937 in Prince Albert, SK, M: 30 Aug 1962 in Sudbury, ON.
63.   ii.   Claudette Audrey Vivian Ethier, B: 17 Feb 1946 in Prince Albert, SK, D: 06 Dec 2006 in Victoria, BC, M: 09 Sep 1966.
    iii.   Ronald Russell Ethier, B: 31 Dec 1940 in Hoey, SK, D: 01 Feb 1941 in Hoey, SK.

23. Lorraine Guillet-3 (Henri Francois Guillet-2, Francois Guillet-1) was born on 29 Dec 1935 in Domremy, SK. She married Arthur Courturier on 29 Oct 1953 in Jean Cote, AB. He was born on 09 Apr 1928 in Lamoureux, AB.

Children of Lorraine Guillet and Arthur Courturier are:
64.   i   Felix Arthur Henry Joseph Courturier, B: 18 Apr 1955 in McLennan, AB, M: 18 Oct 1976 in Dawson Creek, BC.
65.   ii.   Kathleen Marie Bernadette Courturier, B: 17 Jan 1958 in Pouce Coupe, BC, M: 18 Oct 1976 in Joussard, AB.
    iv.   Terry Paul Victor Courturier, B: 15 May 1964 in Fort Nelson, BC.
    v.   Jimmy Dean Courturier, B: 04 Mar 1969 in Dawson Creek, BC.

24. Gabrielle Guillet-3 (Henri Francois Guillet-2, Francois Guillet-1) was born on 01 Apr 1918 in Wakaw, SK. She died on 22 Jul 1980 in Prince Albert, SK. She married Victor Prefontaine on 06 Oct 1939 in Domremy, SK. He was born on 08 Apr 1917 in Prud'homme, SK. He died on 26 Sep 1976 in Kansas City, Missouri, USA.

Children of Gabrielle Guillet and Victor Prefontaine are:

66. i. Daniel Prefontaine, B: 05 Aug 1940 in Prince Albert, SK, M: 24 Aug 1963 in Prince Albert, SK.

67. ii. Sylvia Bertha Marie Prefontaine, B: 09 Nov 1944 in Cudworth, SK, M: 26 Dec 1965 in Blue Spring, Missouri, USA.

25. Agnes Guillet-3 (Eugene Leon Guillet-2, Francois Guillet-1) was born on 22 Sep 1921 in Domremy, SK. She married Joseph Albert Sarrasin. He died in Prince Albert, SK.

Children of Agnes Guillet and Joseph Albert Sarrasin are:

68. i Augustine Sarrasin, B: 05 Mar 1941.
69. ii. Eugene Sarrasin.
70. iii. Lawrence Sarrasin.
71 iv. Elaine Frances Sarrasin, M: 20 Jan 1968.
   v. Evelyn Margaret Sarrasin, M: 05 Jul 1969.
72. vi. Marie Sarrasin.
73. vii. Louise Sarrasin, M: 19 May 1970.
74. viii. Margaret Sarrasin.
75. ix. Jeannette Sarrasin.
76. x. Vivian Sarrasin.

Agnes (Guillet) Sarrasin

Augustine

Agnes (Guillet) Sarrasin Family Back: Louise, Augustine, Eugene, Laurent, Marguerite, Evelyn Front: Jeanette, Agnes, Albert, Vivian and Elaine. Missing from photo: Marie

26. Gilbert Guillet-3 (Eugene Leon Guillet-2, Francois Guillet-1) was born on 13 Nov 1922 in Domremy, SK. He died on 20 Sep 2001 in Domremy, SK. He married Therese Lepine on 26 Oct 1948. She was born in Apr 1929.

Relationship Notes for Therese Lepine and Gilbert Guillet: Grandma Guillet and Octavie were first cousins - making Gilbert and Therese second cousins.

Children of Gilbert Guillet and Therese Lepine are:

77. i.   Carol Marie Guillet, B: 17 May 1949, M: 05 Jul 1968.
78. ii. Rita Guillet, B: 13 May 1953, M: 10 Oct 1970.
     iii. Victor Guillet, B: 12 Apr 1962, M: 26 Aug 1989.
     iv. Denise Guillet, B: 19 Apr 1969, M: 06 Oct 1990.
79. v.   Aline Guillet, B: 19 Jun 1957, M: 05 Aug 1975.
80. vi. Teena Seegerts, B: 08 Jan 1957, M: 05 Jun 1976.

Gilbert Guillet and Family

Marriage Certificate For Gilbert Guillet and Therese Lepine

Gilbert Guillet and family

35

27. Johnny Guillet-3 (Eugene Leon Guillet-2, Francois Guillet-1) was born on 08 Aug 1924 in Domremy, SK. He died on 07 Jan 2000 in Regina, SK. He married Kay Schafeor. She was born on 15 Feb 1928. She died on 04 Jul 2004.

Child of Johnny Guillet and Kay Schafeor is:
81.   i.   Angie Guillet, B: 28 Apr 1947.

Johnny Guillet, Kate, daughter Angie and Grandson

28. Frances Guillet-3 (Eugene Leon Guillet-2, Francois Guillet-1) was born on 08 Jan 1926 in Domremy, SK. She died on 07 Sep 2003 in Regina, SK. She married Leo Paul Marcel Hamel on 21 Sep 1949 in Domremy, SK. He was born on 22 Dec 1917 in Wauchope, SK. He died on 16 Apr 2005 in Regina, SK.

Children of Frances Guillet and Leo Paul Marcel Hamel are:
82.   i.   Evelyn Hamel, B: 03 Jun 1950 in Regina, SK, M: 28 Jan1978 in Regina, SK.
83.   ii.   Jacqueline Jean Hamel, B: 07 Jan 1954 in Regina, SK, M: 06 Mar 1981 in Regina, SK.
84.   iii.   Ronald Robert Hamel, B: 12 Jan 1961 in Regina, SK, M: 10 Nov 1990 in Regina, SK.

Paul and Frances Hamel

*Frances (Guillet) Hamel Family (Back) Robert, Jocelyn, Theodore, Nicholas, David, Jim (middle)
Jacqueline, Elevlyn, Paul (front) Ron, Emilienne, Kiera, and Barbara*

*Evelyn, Paul, Ron,
Frances and Jacqueline*

Paul and Frances Hamel

37

29. Irene Guillet-3 (Eugene Leon Guillet-2, Francois Guillet-1) was born on 12 May 1928 in Domremy, SK. She married Leo Dumont on 24 Nov 1949 in Domremy, SK. He was born on 12 Jan 1930 in Dumas, SK.

Children of Irene Guillet and Leo Dumont are:
85. i.   Roger Jules Eugene Dumont, B: 09 Oct 1950 in Regina, SK, M: 30 Jun 1973 in Regina, SK.
86. ii. Denis Arestride Dumont, B: 13 Feb 1952 in Regina, SK, M: 28 May 1972 in Regina, SK.
87. iii. Lorraine Ann Dumont, B: 28 Nov 1954 in Regina, SK, M: 28 Jun 1975 in Regina, SK.

Irene Dumont and Family

88. iv. Leonard Clement Dumont, B: 17 Aug 1953 in Regina, SK, M: 30 Jul 1983 in Regina, SK.
89. v.   Kenneth John Dumont, B: 22 May 1958 in Regina, SK, M: 09 Oct 1978 in Regina, SK.
90. vi. Rene Ernest Dumont, B: 18 Sep 1959 in Regina, SK, M: 19 Sep 1993 in Regina, SK.
91. vii. Jeannie Dumont, B: 02 Feb 1962 in Regina, SK.
92. viii.Martin John Dumont, B: 14 Oct 1964 in Regina, SK, M: 22 Apr 1995 in North Battleford, SK.

30. Leon Guillet-3 (Eugene Leon Guillet-2, Francois Guillet-1) was born on 08 May 1930 in Domremy, SK. He died on 04 Dec 1999 in Kamloops, BC. He married Mary Janner on 28 Jul 1949 in Regina, SK. She was born on 11 Dec 1929 in Regina, SK. She died on 20 Mar 1981 in Langley, BC.

Children of Leon Guillet and Mary Janner are:

Leo Guillet - 18 years of age

93. i. Darlene Guillet, B: 22 Nov 1949 in Regina, SK, M: 22 Nov 1969.

ii. Irene Guillet, B: 26 Oct 1950 in Regina, SK.

94. iii. Lawrence Guillet, B: 21 Jan 1953 in Regina, SK.

95. iv. Catherine Guillet, B: 04 Jun 1962 in Vancouver, BC.

96. v. Sharon Guillet, B: 07 Feb 1966 in Vancouver, BC, M: 21 May 1988 in Langley, BC.

*Mary (Janner) Guillet
18 years of age*

Lawrence, Darlene, Mary, Leo, Catherine, Irene and Sharon Guillet

Lawrence Darlene, Cousins
Leona and Eugene (Butch)
and Irene

Leo and Mary Guillet

Irene, Darlene, Belinda
and Leona

Mary and Cathy

Cathy

Sharon, (in behind) Darlene, Leo, Lawrence, Irene and Cathy

40

31. Aline Guillet-3 (Eugene Leon Guillet-2,Francois Guillet-1) was born on 26 Mar 1933 in Domremy, SK. She married Albert Joseph Lestage on 07 Apr 1953, son of Henry Lestage and Yvonne. He was born on 08 May 1928 in Albertville, SK. He died on 05 Feb 1990 in Regina, SK.

Children of Aline Guillet and Albert Joseph Lestage are:

97. i.   Roland Albert Lestage, B: 22 Dec 1953 in Regina, SK, M: 24 Aug 1974.
98. ii.   Gary Glenn Lestage,B: 28 Nov 1954 in Regina, SK, M: 31 Jan 1976.

Aline Guillet

99. iii. Claudette Lorette Lestage, B: 01 Jun 1958 in Regina, SK, M: 02 Jan.
     iv.   Gregory Leslie Lestage, B: 04 Jul 1959 in Regina, SK, D: 25 Oct 1978 in Regina, SK.
100. v.   Rodney Drew Lestage, B: 09 May 1965 in Regina, SK, M: 13 Nov 1989.
     vi.   Valerie Angie Lestage, B: 10 Jul 1974 in Regina, SK.

Aline Guillet

Raymond Guillet

32.Raymond Albert Guillet-3 (Eugene Leon Guillet-2, Francois Guillet-1) was born on 06 Sep 1936 in Domremy, SK [2]. He married Marie Annette Greyeyes on 05 Jan 1957 in Vancouver, BC, daughter of William Richard Greyeyes and Bertha Eva Beauchamp. She was born on 03 Feb 1938 in Muskeg Lake Reserve, SK. He married Louise Williams on 30 Dec 1982 in Vancouver, BC. She was born in Trail, BC.

Children of Raymond Albert Guillet
and Marie Annette Greyeyes are:

101. i. Eugene Raymond Guillet,
B: 01 Oct 1956 in
Vancouver, BC, D: 06 Sep
1989 in Surrey, BC, M: 18
Sep 1982 in Delta, BC.

    ii. Leona Frances Guillet,
B: 05 Jul 1958 in
Vancouver, BC, D: 19
Nov 1965 in Vancouver, BC.

102. iii. Belinda Ann Guillet, B: 03
Jul 1959 in Vancouver,
BC, M: 21 Jul 1979 in
Vancouver, BC.

Raymond Guillet

103. iv. Ramona Marie Guillet,
B: 06 Jan 1961 in Vancouver, BC, M: 10 Apr 1982
in Kamloops, BC.

104. v. Elaina Aline Darlene Guillet, B: 26 Sep 1964 in Vancouver,
BC, M: 07 Aug 1982 in Kamloops, BC.

*(Back) Annette, Belinda,
Eugene, Raymond
(Front) Elaina (on Annette's
lap) Leona and Ramona*

Child of Raymond Albert Guillet and Louise Williams is:

    i. Raymond Cecil Guillet. Married Andrea (Unknown)

Certificate of Baptism

I certify that according to the Register of Baptisms at the Church of

St. Andrew at Vancouver, B.C.

Leona Frances Guillet {son / daughter}

of Raymond A. Guillet and Annetta Marie Greyeyes

(formerly), his wife, born July 5, 19 58

was baptized on August 3, 19 58

Godfather Eugene Guillet Priest Father Smeets

Godmother Eva Greyeyes

This 26th day of July, 19 59. (Signed) Rev. H. Smeets

McCready's Printing Co., Tillsonburg, Ont.

Leona Guillet

GUILLET—In hospital November 18, 1965, Leona Frances, aged 7 years, beloved daughter of Raymond and Marie Guillet of 1174 East 33rd Avenue and sister of Belinda, Ramona, Elaina and Eugene. Funeral Mass Monday, November 22 at 10 a.m. in St. Andrews Church, 480 E. 47th Avenue. Rev. D. McInerney, celebrant. Interment Valley View. Kearney Funeral Directors, 1096 W. Broadway. —

33. Marcel Guillet-3 (Louis Guillet-2, Francois Guillet-1) was born on 31 Oct 1922 in Domremy, SK. He died on 14 Oct 1971 in Prince Albert, SK. He met A. Deters.

Children of Marcel Guillet and A. Deters are:
    i. Lawrence Larry Guillet.
    ii. George Guillet, B: 29 Jun.

34. Elise Marie Rollande Guillet-3 (Louis Guillet-2, Francois Guillet-1) was born on 21 Sep 1923 in Wakaw, SK. She married Lawrence Delorme on 23 Sep 1946 in Prince Albert, SK. He was born on 06 Jan 1926 in Prince Albert, SK. He died on 04 Nov 1998 in Prince Albert, SK.

Children of Elise Marie Rollande Guillet and Lawrence Delorme are:
105. i. Gary Delorme, B: 11 Jun 1949 in Prince Albert, SK, M: 01 Mar 1980 in Prince Albert, SK.
106. ii. John Delorme, B: 12 Dec 1952 in Prince Albert, SK, M: 01 May 1971 in Prince Albert, SK.

35. Laura Ethier-3 (Camille Guillet-2, Francois Guillet-1). She married George Kustaski on 01 Mar 1954.

Children of Laura Ethier and George Kustaski are:
107. i. Linda Kustaski.
108. ii. Vern Kustaski.
109. iii. Elaine Kustaski.
    iv. Garry Kustaski.
110. v. Robert Kustaski.
    vi. Colleen Kustaski.
    vii. Lori Ann Kustaski.

36. Andre Ethier-3 (Camille Guillet-2, Francois Guillet-1) was born on 04 Nov 1930. He died on 02 Jun 1981. He married Annette Chernowsky on 1956 in Canora, SK.

  Children of Andre Ethier and Annette Chernowsky are:
    i.   Brian Ethier.
    ii.   Daryl Ethier.
    iii. Colleen Ethier.
    iv.   Colette Ethier.
    v.   Derek Ethier.

37. Clarence Ethier-3 (Camille Guillet-2, Francois Guillet-1) was born on 18 Apr 1941. He married Madeleine Carrier on 04 Nov 1963 in Prince Albert, SK.

  Children of Clarence Ethier and Madeleine Carrier are:
    i.   Lawrence Ethier, B: 31 May 1964.
    ii.   Roger Ethier, B: 12 Oct 1965.
    iii. Kelly Ethier, B: 02 Jan 1969.

GENERATION 4

38. Sharyn Edith Dianne Guillet-4
(Edward Guillet-3, Henri Francois
Guillet-2, Francois Guillet-1) was
born on 14 Jun 1949 in Hudson Bay,
SK. She married Gordon Wayne
Haw on 26 Jul 1969 in Chetwynd,
BC, son of Thomas Albert Haw and
Edna May Carlson. He was born on
14 Mar 1947 in Trail, BC.

Sharyn (Guillet) and Gordon Haw

Children of Sharyn Edith Dianne Guillet and Gordon Wayne Haw are:
111. i.   Nicole Haw, B: 02 May 1970 in Dawson Creek BC, M: Chetwynd, BC.
112. ii. Connie-Jo Haw, B: 13 Jul 1977 in Chetwynd, BC.
     iii. Wayne Albert Haw, B: 14 Feb 1974 in Chetwynd, BC.

39. Dennis Edward Norman Guillet-4 (Edward Guillet-3, Henri Francois Guillet-2, Francois Guillet-1) was born on 18 Jan 1944 in Hudson Bay, SK. He married Linda Mary Hudson on 10 Aug 1968 in Chetwynd, BC, daughter of Floyd Joseph Hudson and Della Mary Durney. She was born on 08 Aug 1950 in Dawson Creek, BC.

Children of Dennis Edward Norman Guillet and Linda Mary Hudson are:
113. i.   Tammy Lynne Guillet, B: 28 Mar 1969 in Dawson Creek, BC.
     ii. Christopher Dennis Guillet, B: 28 Oct 1972 in Fort St. John, BC.
114. iii. Theresa Simone Guillet, B: 26 Nov 1971 in Chetwynd, BC, M: 02 Sep 1995 in Taylor, BC.

40.Ernest Henry Guillet-4 (Edward Guillet-3, Henri Francois Guillet-2, Francois Guillet-1) was born on 20 Sep 1945 in Hudson Bay, SK. He married Dianne Paul on 07 Nov 1964 in Chetwynd, BC, daughter of Nap Paul and Jean. She was born on 10 Aug 1948 in Yellowknife, N.W.T. He married Lorrie Ann Beamish on 10 Jun 1983 in Chetwynd, BC.

Children of Ernest Henry Guillet and Dianne Paul are:
116. i.   Lisa Marie Guillet, B: 06 Feb 1968 in Dawson Creek, BC.
     ii.   Ernest William Edward Guillet, B: 03 Oct 1965 in Dawson Creek, BC, D: 06 May 1998 in Chetwynd, BC.

Children of Ernest Henry Guillet and Lorrie Ann Beamish are:
     i.   Ryan Cyril Guillet, B: 10 Dec 1983 in Chetwynd, BC.
115. ii.   Candice Gail Guillet, B: 06 Jul 1985 in Chetwynd, BC, M: Jul 2005 in Chetwynd, BC.

41. Donald Lorne Guillet-4 (Edward Guillet-3, Henri Francois Guillet-2, Francois Guillet-1) was born on 3 Dec 1946 in Hudson Bay, SK. He married Sharlene Jeanette Seidel on 25 Feb 1967 in Chetwynd, BC, daughter of Clarence William Seidel and Ethel May Affie. She was born on 25 Jun 1951 in Meadow Lake, SK. She died on 28 Dec 1991 in Chetwynd, BC.

Children of Donald Lorne Guillet and Sharlene Jeanette Seidel are:
117. i.   Bridget Jeanette Guillet, B: 06 Sep 1967 in Dawson Creek, BC, M: 20 Jul 1985 in Chetwynd, BC.
118. ii.   Dawn Lee Guillet, B: 14 Oct 1971 in Chetwynd, BC, M: 11 Nov 1994 in Chetwynd, BC.

42. Leslie Gordon Guillet-4 (Edward Guillet-3, Henri Francois Guillet-2, Francois Guillet-1) was born on 08 Oct 1947 in Hudson Bay, SK. He married Winnifred Bibaud. She was born on 06 Apr 1954 in Edmonton, AB.

Children of Leslie Gordon Guillet and Winnifred Bibaud are:
119. i   Maxime Edward Leslie Guillet, B: 25 Aug 1974 in Edmonton, AB, M: 12 Jun 2002 in Harrison Hot Springs, BC.
120. ii. Michael Gordon Jerald Guillet, B: 25 Sep 1977 in Fort St. John, BC.
      iii. Jeannie Lynn Guillet, B: 22 Mar 1982 in Fort St. John, BC.

43. Norman Daryl Guillet-4 (Edward Guillet-3, Henri Francois Guillet-2, Francois Guillet-1) was born 04 Jul 1955 in McLennan, AB. He married Connie Francis Wood on 08 Oct 1977 in Chetwynd, BC, daughter of Kenneth Lauren Wood and Phyllis Charlotte MacDougall. She was born on 06 Jan 1958.

Children of Norman Daryl Guillet and Connie Francis Wood are:
121. i.   Collin Rene Guillet, B: 27 Feb 1980 in Chetwynd, BC.
     ii. Brandy Rae Guillet,B: 19 Jun 1981 in Chetwynd, BC.

44. Sandra Lynn Guillet-4 (Edward Guillet-3, Henri Francois Guillet-2, Francois Guillet-1) was born on 31 Jul 1958 in Dawson Creek, BC. She married Robert James Shevkenek on 16 Oct 1976. He was born on 01 Dec 1956 in Chetwynd, BC. She married Richard Beattie on 25 Jul 2003 in Dawson Creek, BC, son of William Dale Joseph Hugh Beattie and Olive Marie Westgate. He was born on 25 Sep 1959 in Pouce Coupe, BC.

Sandra and Richard Beattie

Children of Sandra Lynn Guillet and Robert James Shevkenek are:
122. i.   Loni James Shevkenek, B: 22 Mar 1977 in Chetwynd, BC.
123. ii. Trudy Lynn Shevkenek, B: 30 Aug 1978 in Fort St. John, BC.

45. Janice Laurelle Guillet-4 (Edward Guillet-3, Henri Francois Guillet-2, Francois Guillet-1) was born on 03 Jun 1960 in Dawson Creek, BC. She married Mervine Lorne Spiers on 09 Oct 1982.

Children of Janice Laurelle Guillet and Mervine Lorne Spiers are:
i.   Cale Lorne Spiers, B: 12 Jul 1983 in Dawson Creek, BC.
ii. Devon Nancy Spiers, B: 24 Aug 1989 in Dawson Creek, BC.

46. Edward Maurice Guillet Jr. 4 (Edward Guillet-3, Henri Francois Guillet-2, Francois Guillet-1) was born on 10 Oct 1961 in Dawson Creek, BC. He married Penny McQuigge on 26 Jul 1986 in Chetwynd, BC. He met Melanie Gladys Joy James, daughter of Kenneth James and Donna Patricia Lindstrom. She was born on 30 Sep 1970 in Drayton Valley, AB.

Children of Edward Maurice Guillet Jr. and Penny McQuigge are:
i.   Tyler James Guillet, B: 30 Apr 1986 in Chetwynd, BC.
ii. Travis Edward David Guillet, B: 05 Mar 1988 in Chetwynd, BC.

Children of Edward Maurice Guillet Jr. and Melanie Gladys Joy James are:
i.   Ella Violet Joy Guillet, B: 02 Jan 2004 in Fort St. John, BC.
ii. Evan Kenneth Edward Guillet, B: 10 Aug 2006 in Chetwynd, BC.

Edward, Melanie and Ella Guillet 2004

47. Kevin Joseph Guillet-4 (Edward Guillet-3, Henri Francois Guillet-2, Francois Guillet-1) was born on 10 Apr 1965 in Dawson Creek, BC. He married Vicky Helen Moore on 30 Mar 1985 in Chetwynd, BC. She was born on 23 Nov 1964 in Dawson Creek, BC.

   Children of Kevin Joseph Guillet and Vicky Helen Moore are:
   i. Ashley Irene Ida Guillet, B: 15 Sep 1985 in Chetwynd, BC.
   ii. Shelbie Audrianna Guillet, B: 14 Mar 1990 in Chetwynd, BC.
   iii. Tanner Gary Guillet, B: 23 Aug 1991 in Chetwynd, BC.
   iv. Cory John Heroux, B: 07 Sep 1994 in Terrace, BC.

48. Dorina Guillet-4 (Clement Guillet-3, Henri Francois Guillet-2, Francois Guillet-1) was born on 03 Sep 1946 in Cudworth, SK. She married Terry Mareschal on 31 Aug 1968 in Domremy, SK. He was born on 02 Jun 1945 in Cudworth, SK.

   Children of Dorina Guillet and Terry Mareschal are:
   i. Renee Mareschal, B: 11 May 1972 in Regina, SK, M: 18 Jul 1998.
   ii. Warren Mareschal, B: 18 Nov 1974 in Regina, SK, M: 06 Mar 1999.

49. Gerald Guillet-4 (Clement Guillet-3, Henri Francois Guillet-2, Francois Guillet-1) was born on 27 Jul 1949 in Cudworth, SK. He married Joyce Tobin on 01 Sep 1973 in Birsay, SK. She was born on 11 Apr 1951 in Delisle, SK.

   Children of Gerald Guillet and Joyce Tobin are:
   i. Chantelle Guillet, B: 09 Oct 1976 in Saskatoon, SK.
   ii. Andre Victor Guillet, B: 07 May 1979 in Saskatoon, SK.
   iii. Danielle Lynn Guillet, B: 20 Aug 1982.

50. Lucille M. Guillet-4 (Clement Guillet-3, Henri Francois Guillet-2, Francois Guillet-1) was born on 10 Feb 1951 in Cudworth, SK. She married Michael Pylypchuk on 03 Jul 1976 in Domremy, SK He was born on 23 Jul 1952 in Leoville, SK.

> Children of Lucille M. Guillet and Michael Pylypchuk are:
> i.   Dean Curtis Pylypchuk, B: 23 Jan 1982 in Saskatoon, SK.
> ii. Leanne Michelle Pylypchuk, B: 01 Feb 1986 in Saskatoon, SK.

51. Robert Guillet-4 (Clement Guillet-3, Henri Francois Guillet-2, Francois Guillet-1) was born on 17 May 1952 in Cudworth, SK. He married Etta Duff on 03 Jul 1976 in a double wedding with Lucille and Michael. She was born on 10 Jun 1952 in Aberdeenshire, Scotland.

> Children of Robert Guillet and Etta Duff are:
> i.   Lisa Marie Guillet, B: 25 Jul 1981 in Surrey, BC.
> ii. Michelle Marie Guillet, B: 09 Jan 1986 in Surrey, BC.

52. Maurice Guillet-4 (Clement Guillet-3, Henri Francois Guillet-2, Francois Guillet-1) was born on 24 Jun 1959 in Wakaw, SK. He married Andrea Marie Szabo on 06 Aug 1988. She was born on 24 Sep 1959 in Prince Albert, SK.

> Child of Maurice Guillet and Andrea Marie Szabo is:
> i.   Michelle Clement Guillet, B: 02 Aug 1990 in Prince Albert, SK.

53. Mark Harold Guillet-4 (Clement Guillet-3, Henri Francois Guillet-2, Francois Guillet-1) was born on 18 Nov 1963 in Wakaw, SK. He married Janet Vedress on 25 Apr 1992. She was born on 20 Dec in Saskatoon, SK.

> Children of Mark Harold Guillet and Janet Vedress are:
> i.   Kyle Luc Guillet, B: 01 Apr 1993 in Prince Albert, SK.
> ii. Andrea Vandrees Guillet, B: 12 May 1982.
> iii. Collin Bradly Guillet, B: 11 May 1995 in Regina, SK.

54. Daniel Guillet-4 (Felix Guillet-3, Henri Francois Guillet-2, Francois Guillet-1) was born on 13 Mar 1950 in Domremy, SK.He died on 22 Aug 2004. He married Jane Mercredi on 12 May 1973 in Yellowknife, NWT. She was born on 12 May 1955 in Yellowknife, NWT.

Child of Daniel Guillet and Jane Mercredi is:
  i.   Christine Guillet, B: 16 Nov 1974 in Yellowknife, NWT.

55. Linda Guillet-4 (Felix Guillet-3, Henri Francois Guillet-2, Francois Guillet-1) was born on 27 Jun 1958 in Domremy, SK. She married Maurice Guillet on 18 Dec 1975 in Nipawin, SK. He was born on 01 Jan 1957 in Nipawin, SK.

Children of Linda Guillet and Maurice Guillet are:
  i.   Christopher Guillet, B: 19 Apr 1976 in Nipawin, SK, D: 15 Feb 1997.
  ii. Scott Guillet, B: 16 Mar 1978 in Nipawin, SK.

56. Anita Marie Cecile Ethier-4 (Henriette Guillet-3, Henri Francois Guillet-2, Francois Guillet-1) was born on 19 Sep 1937 in Prince Albert, SK. She married Hector Comeau on 27 Oct 1953 in Marie Reine, AB. He was born on 02 Jan 1931.

Children of Anita Marie Cecile Ethier and Hector Comeau are:
  124. i.   Gerald Paul Comeau, B: 24 Oct 1954 in Peace River, AB, M: 14 Jul 1984 in Edmonton, AB.
  125. ii. Richard Louise Comeau, B: 31 Aug 1955 in Peace River, AB, M: 03 Nov 1973 in Peace River, BC.
  126. iii. Victor Phillip Comeau, B: 09 Aug 1956 in Peace River, AB, M: 02 Aug 1975 in Peace River, BC.
  127. iv. Denise Raymond Comeau, B: 17 Nov 1957 in Peace River, AB, M: 20 Mar 1982.
  128. v.   Claude Eugene Comeau, B: 26 Jan 1959 in Fort St. John, BC, D: 15 May 1981 in High Prairie, AB.

129. vi. Claudette Marie Dianne Comeau, B: 28 Apr 1960 in Peace River, AB, D: 29 Oct 1998 in Peace River, AB, M: 21 Oct 1978 in Rose Valley, SK.

vii. Norman Hector Comeau, B: 19 May 1961 in Maire Reine, AB, D: 29 May 1964 in Maire Reine, AB.

130. viii. Roger Comeau, B: 14 Jan 1963.

131. ix. Michael Patrick Comeau, B: 03 Jul 1964 in Peace River, AB, M: 23 May 1987.

57. Edward Charles Maurice Ethier-4 (Henriette Guillet-3, Henri Francois Guillet-2, Francois Guillet-1) was born on 06 Jan 1939 in St. Louis, SK. He married Betty Zayha-Aseltine on 31 May 1969 in Dawson Creek, BC. She was born on 17 Oct 1937 in Spirit River, AB. She died on 19 Sep 1991 in Chetwynd, BC.

Children of Edward Charles Maurice Ethier and Betty Zayha-Aseltine are:
    i. William Wayne Ethier, B: 12 Jan 1958 in Dawson Creek, BC.
    ii. Larry Wade Ethier, B: 08 Jan 1961 in
    iii. Blaine Allan Ethier, B: 03 Mar 1970 in Dawson Creek, BC, M: 29 Aug 1998 in Chetwynd, BC.
132. iv. Brian Edward Ethier, B: 03 Mar 1970 in Dawson Creek, BC, M: 23 Aug 1997 in Chetwynd, BC.

58. Denise Marie Ethier-4 (Henriette Guillet-3, Henri Francois Guillet-2, Francois Guillet-1) was born on 18 May 1944 in Prince Albert. She married Peter Podolecki on 28 Oct 1961 in Chetwynd, BC. He was born on 02 Jun 1939 in Vermillion, AB. She married Joseph Arthur Gray on 25 Oct 1982. He died on 31 Mar 1992.

Children of Denise Marie Ethier and Peter Podolecki are:
133. i. Patricia Anne Podolecki, B: 03 May 1962 in Dawson Creek, BC, M: 09 Feb 1985 in Chetwynd, BC.
134. ii. Michael Peter Podolecki, B: 01 Apr 1963 in Williams Lake, BC, M: 02 Jul 1988 in Chetwynd, BC.

iii. Richard Matthew Podolecki, B: 06 Jun 1964 in Williams Lake, BC.
iv. Teresa Podolecki, B: 27 Jul 1965 in Williams Lake, BC.

59. Leo Ethier-4 (Henriette Guillet-3, Henri Francois Guillet-2, Francois Guillet-1) was born on 29 Jul 1945 in Prince Albert, SK. He married Nancy Hanusz on 14 Oct 1966 in Peace River, BC. She was born on 24 Oct 1946 in Peace River, AB.

Children of Leo Ethier and Nancy Hanusz are:
i. Curtis Wade Ethier, B: 17 Mar 1971 in Peace River, AB, M: 30 Jul 1994 in Grande Prairie, AB.
ii. Jeffrey Mark Ethier, B: 18 Jan 1975 in Peace River, AB, M: 15 Aug 1998 in Peace River, BC.

60. Maurice Joseph Ethier-4 (Henriette Guillet-3, Henri Francois Guillet-2, Francois Guillet-1) was born on 21 Apr 1949 in Prince Albert, SK. He married Evelyne Carlick on 14 Jun 1975 in Chetwynd, BC. She was born on 31 Jul 1951 in Cassiar, BC.

Children of Maurice Joseph Ethier and Evelyne Carlick are:
i. Sean Colin Ethier, B: 17 May 1971 in Cassiar, BC.
ii. Christopher Colin Ethier, B: 20 Jun 1972 in Williams Lake, BC.

61. Aline Marie Ethier-4 (Henriette Guillet-3, Henri Francois Guillet-2, Francois Guillet-1) was born on 29 Jul 1951 in Peace River, BC. She married Edward Wittstruck on 08 Aug 1970 in Chetwynd, BC. He was born on 04 Oct 1951 in Edmonton, AB.

Children of Aline Marie Ethier and Edward Wittstruck are:
i. Kenneth James Wittstruck, B: 01 Jul 1969, D: 01 Jul 1969; was stillborn.

135. ii. Colin James Wittstruck, B: 20 Aug 1973 in Fort St. John, BC, M:15 Jul 1995.

      iii. Jason Edward Wittstruck, B: 14 Jun 1976.

62. Leonard Ronald Ethier-4 (Alice Gabrielle Guillet-3, Henri Francois Guillet-2, Francois Guillet-1) was born on 03 Oct 1937 in Prince Albert, SK. He married Marjorie Rae Moxam on 30 Aug 1962 in Sudbury, ON. She was born on 02 Feb 1940 in Gatchell, ON.

Child of Leonard Ronald Ethier and Marjorie Rae Moxam is:
136. i. Connie Lee Ethier, B: 17 Nov 1965 in Sudbury, ON.

63. Claudette Audrey Vivian Ethier-4 (Alice Gabrielle Guillet-3, Henri Francois Guillet-2, Francois Guillet-1) was born on 17 Feb 1946 in Prince Albert, SK. She died on 06 Dec 2006 in Victoria, BC. She married Brian Beaudry on 09 Sep 1966. He was born on 02 Mar 1946 in Regina, SK.

Child of Claudette Audrey Vivian Ethier and Brian Beaudry is:
     i. Brian Scott Beaudry, B: 23 Mar 1967 in Windsor, ON.

64. Felix Arthur Henry Joseph Courturier-4 (Lorraine Guillet-3, Henri Francois Guillet-2, Francois Guillet-1) was born on 18 Apr 1955 in McLennan, AB. He married Sharon Ann Purschke on 18 Oct 1976 in Dawson Creek, BC. She was born on 16 Oct 1958 in St. Albert, AB.

Child of Felix Arthur Henry Joseph Courturier and Sharon Ann Purschke is:
     i. April Ann Courturier, B: 25 Jan 1978 in Dawson Creek, BC.

65. Kathleen Marie Bernadette Courturier-4 (Lorraine Guillet-3, Henri Francois Guillet-2, Francois Guillet-1) was born on 17 Jan 1958 in Pouce Coupe, BC. She married Richard Couturier on 18 Oct 1976 in Joussard, AB. He was born on 15 Aug 1959 in McLennan, AB.

Children of Kathleen Marie Bernadette Courturier and Richard Couturier are:
    i.   Martina Couturier, B: 22 Dec 1974 in Dawson Creek, BC.
    ii.   Jeanette Couturier, B: 16 Apr 1978 in Peace River, AB.
    iii. Madelene Couturier, B: 29 Sep 1979 in Peace River, AB.

66. Daniel Prefontaine-4 (Gabrielle Guillet-3, Henri Francois Guillet-2, Francois Guillet-1) was born on 5 Aug 1940 in Prince Albert, SK. He married Marguerite Charlebois on 24 Aug 1963 in Prince Albert, SK. She was born on 12 Apr 1942 in Marcelin, SK.

Children of Daniel Prefontaine and Marguerite Charlebois are:
       i.   Nicole Prefontaine, B: 22 Nov 1964 in Prince Albert, SK, M: 28 Jul 1990 in Ottawa, ON.
137. ii.   Lisa Prefontaine, B: 15 Dec 1965 in Prince Albert, SK, M: 18 Aug 1995 in Ottawa, ON.
      iii. Rachelle Prefontaine, B: 26 Feb 1968 in Prince Albert, SK.

67. Sylvia Bertha Marie Prefontaine-4 (Gabrielle Guillet-3, Henri Francois Guillet-2, Francois Guillet-1) was born on 09 Nov 1944 in Cudworth, SK. She married John Bowman Nelson on 26 Dec 1965 in Blue Spring, Missouri, USA. He was born on 09 Nov 1944 in Kansas City, Missouri, USA.

Children of Sylvia Bertha Marie Prefontaine and John Bowman Nelson are:
138. i.   Michelle Marie Nelson, B: 01 Jan 1972 in Kansas City, Missouri, USA.
139. ii. Michel Victor Nelson, B: 25 Oct 1977 in Excelsior Springs, Missouri, USA.

68. Augustine Sarrasin-4 (Agnes Guillet-3, Eugene Leon Guillet-2, Francois Guillet-1) was born on 05 Mar 1941. She married Art Lestage. He was born on 02 Nov 1931.

—Voldeng's
MR. AND MRS. ARTHUR LESTAGE

St. Mark's Church, Scene Of Sarrasin, Lestage Marriage

St. Mark's Church, was the scene of a pretty wedding on June 4, when Father Castelyns, performed the ceremony which united in holy matrimony, Augustine, daughter of Mr. and Mrs. Albert Sarrasin of Prince Albert and Arthur, son of Mr. and Mrs. Henry Lestage of Albertville.

Given in marriage by her father the bride was lovely in a waltz length gown covered with ruffles of lace, the top featured a bolero, with lily point sleeves and tiny button front. Her chapel veil was held in place by a lace headdress. She carried a bouquet of variegated roses, with streamers dotted with rose buds.

Ann Stankowsky as maid of honor chose an apricot short sleeved waltz length gown and carried a bouquet of yellow roses on yellow background. The

bridesmaid, Phyllis Lestage wore a nile green short sleeved waltz length gown and carried a bouquet of pink roses on green background. The petite flower girl, Louise Sarrasin wore a floor length gown of yellow net with a sequined yellow head dress, she carried a bouquet of orange roses on yellow background.

Attending the groom as best man were Bob Lestage and Eugene Sarrasin, while ushering the guests to their pews were, Laurent Sarrasin and Ernest Chenier.

For her daughter's wedding the bride's mother chose a white dress with pink roses, while the groom's mother wore a beige dress with pink flowers.

Toast to the bride was given by the bride's brother, Eugene Sarrasin.

Children of Augustine Sarrasin and Art Lestage are:
  i.   Dale Lestage, B:20 Jun 1962.
  ii. Deanna Lestage, B: 15 Aug 1960.
140. iii. David Lestage, B:03 Oct 1963.
  iv. Dwayne Lestage, B: 01 Jan 1966.
  v.   Darrell Lestage, B: 03 Oct 1963.

69. Eugene Sarrasin-4 (Agnes Guillet-3, Eugene Leon Guillet-2, Francois Guillet-1) He married Rose Mary Davies.

Children of Eugene Sarrasin and Rose Mary Davies are:
  i.   Dorothy Sarrasin.
  ii. Jo-Lan Sarrasin.
  iii. (Girl) Sarrasin.
  iv. (Girl1) Sarrasin.

70. Lawrence Sarrasin-4 (Agnes Guillet-3, Eugene Leon Guillet-2, Francois Guillet-1). He married Evelyn (Unknown).

Children of Lawrence Sarrasin and Evelyn (Unknown) are:
   i.   Kevin Sarrasin.
  ii. Jackie Sarrasin.

71. Elaine Frances Sarrasin-4 (Agnes Guillet-3, Eugene Leon Guillet-2, Francois Guillet-1). She married William Gorden Ferguson on 20 Jan 1968.

Children of Elaine Frances Sarrasin and William Gorden Ferguson are:
    i.   Elaine Ferguson.
   ii. Darleen Ferguson.
  iii. Carolyne Ferguson.
  iv. William Ferguson.

72. Marie Sarrasin-4 (Agnes Guillet-3, Eugene Leon Guillet-2, Francois Guillet-1). She married Bruce Ferguson.

Children of Marie Sarrasin and Bruce Ferguson are:
141. i.   Laurie Ann Ferguson.
142. ii. Scott Ferguson, B: 1969.

73. Louise Sarrasin-4 (Agnes Guillet-3, Eugene Leon Guillet-2, Francois Guillet-1). She married Emile Phaneuf on 19 May 1970.

Children of Louise Sarrasin and Emile Phaneuf are:
   i.   Meka Joseph Phaneuf, B: 05 Sep 1974.
  ii. Mia Phaneuf, B: 1972.

Meka Phaneuf

58

74. Margaret Sarrasin-4 (Agnes Guillet-3, Eugene Leon Guillet-2, Francois Guillet-1). She married Jim Weber.

Child of Margaret Sarrasin and Jim Weber is:
i. Daniel Lawrence Weber, B: 27 Jul 1990.

75. Jeannette Sarrasin-4 (Agnes Guillet-3, Eugene Leon Guillet-2, Francois Guillet-1). She married Mr. Ross.

Child of Jeannette Sarrasin and Mr. Ross is:
i. Kerry Louise Ross, B: Jan 1978.

76. Vivian Sarrasin-4 (Agnes Guillet-3, Eugene Leon Guillet-2, Francois Guillet-1). She married Dave Young.

Child of Vivian Sarrasin and Dave Young is:
i. Alexander Sage Young, B: 03 Jan 1991.

77. Carol Marie Guillet-4 (Gilbert Guillet-3, Eugene Leon Guillet-2, Francois Guillet-1) was born on 17 May 1949. She married Arne Hoffensetz on 05 Jul 1968.

Children of Carol Marie Guillet and Arne Hoffensetz are:
i. Bonnie Marie Hoffensetz, B: 02 Dec 1976.
ii. Dean Hoffensetz, B: 03 Oct 1971.

78. Rita Guillet-4 (Gilbert Guillet-3, Eugene Leon Guillet-2, Francois Guillet-1) was born on 13 May 1953. She married Arsene Emile Billo on 10 Oct 1970.

Children of Rita Guillet and Arsene Emile Billo are:
i. Keith Billo, B: 31 Aug 1973.
ii. Devon Billo, B: 06 Jul 1976.
iii. Kachelle Billo, B: 28 Mar 1986.

79. Aline Guillet-4 (Gilbert Guillet-3, Eugene Leon Guillet-2, Francois Guillet-1) was born on 19 Jun 1957. She married Hubert Remi Rabut on 05 Aug 1975.

Children of Aline Guillet and Hubert Remi Rabut are:
i. Tammy Robert, B: 07 May 1979.
ii. Leanne Robert, B: 16 Nov 1981.
iii. Darcy Robert, B: 15 Aug 1985.

80. Teena Seegerts-4 (Gilbert Guillet-3, Eugene Leon Guillet-2, Francois Guillet-1) was born on 08 Jan 1957. She married Edwin Lyle Hegedus on 05 Jun 1976.

Notes for Teena Seegerts: Teena came from Uranium City and was seven years old when she came to live with the Guillet Family as a foster child 1963 to 1975.

Children of Teena Seegerts and Edwin Lyle Hegedus are:
i. Bryan Hegedus, B: 03 Mar 1977.
ii. Ryan Hegedus, B: 27 May 1979.

81. Angie Guillet-4 (Johnny Guillet-3, Eugene Leon Guillet-2, Francois Guillet-1) was born on 28 Apr 1947. She married John D'Andrea.

Child of Angie Guillet and John D'Andrea is:
i. Troy D'Andrea.

82. Evelyn Hamel-4 (Frances Guillet-3, Eugene Leon Guillet-2, Francois Guillet-1) was born on 03 Jun 1950 in Regina, SK. She married Roger Allan Treland on 28 Jan 1978 in Regina, SK. He was born on 01 Mar 1953. He died on 10 Mar 1995 in Regina, SK.

Children of Evelyn Hamel and Roger Allan Treland are:
i. Nicholas Alexander Treland, B: 27 Feb 1983.
ii. David Anthony Treland, B: 11 Mar 1986.

83. Jacqueline Jean Hamel-4 (Frances Guillet-3, Eugene Leon Guillet-2, Francois Guillet-1) was born on 07 Jan 1954 in Regina, SK. She married James Nodge on 06 Mar 1981 in Regina, SK. He was born on 09 Dec 1953.

Children of Jacqueline Jean Hamel and James Nodge are:
   i.   Jocelyn Jean Nodge, B: 17 Aug1983.
   ii. Theodore James Nodge, B: 08Apr 1985.
   iii. Robert Paul Nodge, B: 23 Dec 1987.

84. Ronald Robert Hamel-4 (Frances Guillet-3, Eugene Leon Guillet-2, Francois Guillet-1) was born on 12 Jan 1961 in Regina, SK. He married Barbara Ann Pacholik on 10 Nov 1990 in Regina, SK. She was born on 23 Oct 1965.

Children of Ronald Robert Hamel and Barbara Ann Pacholik are:
   i.   Emilenne Bell Hamel, B: 02 Mar 1999.
   ii. Kiera Julianne Hamel, B: 09 Nov 2001.

Emilie Hamel   *Kiera Hamel*

85. Roger Jules Eugene Dumont-4 (Irene Guillet-3, Eugene Leon Guillet-2, Francois Guillet-1) was born on 09 Oct 1950 in Regina, SK. He married Erica Ann Stamnschroer on 30 Jun 1973 in Regina, SK. She was born on 22 Aug 1953 in Ontario.

Children of Roger Jules Eugene Dumont and Erica Ann Stamnschroer are:
143. i.   Jessica Dumont, B: 28 Jan 1977 in Regina, SK, M: 12 Aug 2000 in Regina, SK.
      ii. Zac Dumont, B: 13 Jun 1982.

86. Denis Arestride Dumont-4 (Irene Guillet-3, Eugene Leon Guillet-2, Francois Guillet-1) was born on 13 Feb 1952 in Regina, SK. He married Judy Licthenwald on 28 May 1972 in Regina, SK. She was born on 11 Sep 1952.

Children of Denis Arestride Dumont and Judy Licthenwald are:
144. i.   Michele Dumont, B: 09 Dec 1974, M: 13 Aug in Regina, SK.
       ii. Leslie Dumont, B: 28 Apr 1977, M: 02 Jun 2001 in Regina, SK.

87. Lorraine Ann Dumont-4 (Irene Guillet-3, Eugene Leon Guillet-2, Francois Guillet-1) was born on 28 Nov 1954 in Regina, SK. She married Colin Chuck Watson on 28 Jun 1975 in Regina, SK. He was born on 22 Oct 1952. She married Eric Nelson on 29 Jul 1998 in Regina, SK. He was born on 22 Aug 1953.

Children of Lorraine Ann Dumont and Colin Chuck Watson are:
       i.   Colleen Watson, B: 01 Jun 1980.
       ii. Brent Watson, B: 06 Feb 1982.

88. Leonard Clement Dumont-4 (Irene Guillet-3, Eugene Leon Guillet-2, Francois Guillet-1) was born on 17 Aug 1953 in Regina, SK. He married Joyce Ann Chaban on 30 Jul 1983 in Regina, SK. She was born on 02 Dec 1954 in Regina, SK.

Children of Leonard Clement Dumont and Joyce Ann Chaban are:
       i.   Adam Dumont, B: 03 Nov 1984.
       ii. Ryan Dumont, B: 18 Jul 1988.

89. Kenneth John Dumont-4 (Irene Guillet-3, Eugene Leon Guillet-2, Francois Guillet-1) was born on 22 May 1958 in Regina, SK. He married Loreen Parker on 09 Oct 1978 in Regina, SK. She was born on 25 Apr 1958 in Kipling.

Children of Kenneth John Dumont and Loreen Parker are:
    i.   Travis Dumont, B: 16 Apr 1986.
    ii.   Marisa Dumont, B: 08 Aug 1989.

90. Rene Ernest Dumont-4 (Irene Guillet-3, Eugene Leon Guillet-2, Francois Guillet-1) was born on 18 Sep 1959 in Regina, SK. He married Trish Elkhorn on 19 Sep 1993 in Regina, SK. She was born on 09 Mar 1964.

Children of Rene Ernest Dumont and Trish Elkhorn are:
    i.   Aurel Dumont, B: 28 Nov 1996.
    ii.   Camille Dumont, B: 14 Jun 1999.

91. Jeannie Dumont-4 (Irene Guillet-3, Eugene Leon Guillet-2, Francois Guillet-1) was born on 02 Feb 1962 in Regina, SK. She married Jeff Ferraton on 09 Oct 1983. He was born on 22 Jun 1962. She married Wayne Tedlock on 05 Aug 2001 in Regina, SK.

    i.   Loretta Dumont, B: 14 May 1980.

Child of Jeannie Dumont and Jeff Ferraton are:
    i.   Brandon Ferraton, B: 22 Jul 1986.

Child of Jeannie Dumont and Wayne Tedlock is:
    i.   Levi Tedlock, B: 07 Dec 2001.

92. Martin John Dumont-4 (Irene Guillet-3, Eugene Leon Guillet-2, Francois Guillet-1) was born on 14 Oct 1964 in Regina, SK. He married Denna Farmer on 22 Apr 1995 in North Battleford, SK. She was born on 19 Feb 1965.

Martin John Dumont

Dekota and Aiden Dumont

Children of Martin John Dumont and Denna Farmer are:
  i.   Dekota Dumont, B: 14 Dec 1998.
  ii. Aiden Dumont, B: 14 Jun 2000.

93. Darlene Guillet-4 (Leon Guillet-3, Eugene Leon Guillet-2, Francois Guillet-1) was born on 22 Nov 1949 in Regina SK. She married Wayne Clark on 22 Nov 1969. She married Allan Pounder in Kamloops, BC. on 08 Sept 2001.

Children of Darlene Guillet and Wayne Clark are:
145. i.   Donna Clark, B: 16 Sept 1975.
146. ii. William Clark, B: 21 Jul 1974.

Darlene Pounder

Irene Guillet-(Leon Guillet-3, Eugene Leon Guillet-2, Francois Guillet-1), B: 26 Oct 1950 in Regina, SK. Common law partner since 17 Oct 1987 with Judith Ellen Jacobson, B: 17 Jul 1946.

Irene Guillet and partner Judith Ellen Jacobson.

Irene Guillet

94. Lawrence Guillet-4 (Leon Guillet-3, Eugene Leon Guillet-2, Francois Guillet-1) was born on 21 Jan 1953 in Regina, SK. He met Donna Wilson, daughter of Doreen Wilson. He married Sandra Joan Robertson on 07 Apr 1973.

Child of Lawrence Guillet and Donna Wilson is:
147. i.   Cindy Darlene Guillet, B: 17 Aug 1978 in Vancouver, BC, M: 01 Apr 2006 in Edmonton, AB.

Lawrence Guillet

95. Catherine Guillet-4 (Leon Guillet-3, Eugene Leon Guillet-2, Francois Guillet-1) was born on 04 Jun 1962 in Vancouver, BC. She married Vince Andrea Viola on 14 Jul 1984. She later married Dean (Unknown).

Child of Catherine Guillet and Vince Andrea Viola is:
i.   Jenny Viola, B: 21 Jan.

Cathy

Jenny

96. Sharon Guillet-4 (Leon Guillet-3, Eugene Leon Guillet-2, Francois Guillet-1) was born on 07 Feb 1966 in Vancouver, BC. She married Jeff Hall on 21 May 1988 in Langley, BC. He was born on 26 Sep 1966 in Langley, BC.

Children of Sharon Guillet and Jeff Hall are:
i. Jesse Hall, B: 19 Jan 1991 in Kamloops, BC.
ii. Lucus Hall, B: 14 Feb 1994 in Kamloops, BC.

Sharon and Jeff Hall

Lucas Hall   *Jesse Hall*

97. Roland Albert Lestage-4 (Aline Guillet-3, Eugene Leon Guillet-2, Francois Guillet-1) was born on 22 Dec 1953 in Regina, SK. He married Debra Joan Hauk on 24 Aug 1974. Later Roland married Pat Maiser.

Child of Roland Albert Lestage and Debra Joan Hauk is:
i. Ryan Lestage, B: 20 Jul 1977.

98. Gary Glenn Lestage-4 (Aline Guillet-3, Eugene Leon Guillet-2, Francois Guillet-1) was born on 28 Nov 1954 in Regina, SK. He married Deborah Ann Kyle on 31 Jan 1976.

Children of Gary Glenn Lestage and Deborah Ann Kyle are:
 i.   Nola Lestage, B: 30 Jul 1976.
 ii. Darcy Lestage, B: 06 Aug 1980.

99. Claudette Lorette Lestage-4 (Aline Guillet-3, Eugene Leon Guillet-2, Francois Guillet-1) was born on 01 Jun 1958 in Regina, SK. She married Douglas Petz on 02 Jan.

Children of Claudette Lorette Lestage and Douglas Petz are:
148. i.   Angeline Petz, B: 02 Feb 1976.
149. ii. Derek Petz, B: 13 Dec 1979.

100. Rodney Drew Lestage-4(Aline Guillet-3, Eugene Leon Guillet-2, Francois Guillet-1) was born on 09 May 1965 in Regina, SK. He married Terri Gartner on 13 Nov 1989.

Children of Rodney Drew Lestage and Terri Gartner are:
 i.   Damond James Lestage, B: 23 Apr 1991.
 ii. Kayleigh Lestage, B: 13 Nov 1988, D: 09 Dec 1988 in Crib death.

101. Eugene Raymond Guillet-4(Raymond Albert Guillet-3, Eugene Leon Guillet-2, Francois Guillet-1) was born on 01 Oct 1956 in Vancouver, BC. He died on 06 Sep 1989 in Surrey, BC. He married Ingrid Abolis on 18 Sep 1982 in Delta, BC.

Child of Eugene Raymond Guillet and Ingrid Abolis is:
 i.   Corey James Guillet, B: 22 May 1987 in Delta, BC.

102. Belinda Ann Guillet-4(Raymond Albert Guillet-3, Eugene Leon Guillet-2, Francois Guillet-1) was born on 03 Jul 1959 in Vancouver, BC. She married

Charles Edward Denness on 21 Jul 1979 in Vancouver, BC, son of Frederick Denness and Joyce Rowe. He was born on 19 Feb 1959 in Charlotte Town, PEI.

Child of Belinda Ann Guillet and Charles Edward Denness is:

150. i. Steven Fredrick Denness, B: 09 Jan 1981 in Vancouver, BC.

Steven Denness

103. Ramona Marie Guillet-4 (Raymond Albert Guillet-3, Eugene Leon Guillet-2, Francois Guillet-1) was born on 06 Jan 1961 in Vancouver, BC. She married Brian William George Davidson on 10 Apr 1982 in Kamloops, BC, son of James Robertson Davidson and Adeline Elsie Batke. He was born on 20 Oct 1960 in Langenburg, SK.

Children of Ramona Marie Guillet and Brian William George Davidson are:

151. i. Tanya Ann Davidson, B: 28 Sept 1982 in Kamloops, BC, M: 02 Aug 2003 in Chetwynd, BC.
152. ii. Jamie Lynn Davidson, B: 03 Jun 1984 in Kamloops, BC, M: 03 Jul 2010 in Chetwynd, BC.

Tanya and Jamie

68

104.Elaina Aline Darlene Guillet-4(Raymond Albert Guillet-3, Eugene Leon Guillet-2, Francois Guillet-1) was born on 26 Sep 1964 in Vancouver, BC. She married Larry Grant Davidson on 7 Aug 1982 in Kamloops, BC, son of James Robertson Davidson and Adeline Elsie Batke. He was born on 07 Mar 1962 in Esterhazy, SK.

Matt Davidson   *Ashley Davidson*
2009 Graduation Calgary
Bachelor of Arts Degree

Children of Elaina Aline Darlene Guillet and Larry Grant Davidson are:
    i.   Alicia Davidson, B. 26 Sep 1983 in Golden BC, D: 26 Sep 1983 in Golden BC, at birth.
    ii.   Ashley Marie Davidson, B: 18 Feb 1987 in Kamloops, BC.
    iii.   Mathew James Ray Davidson, B: 07 Jun 1989 in Kamloops, BC.

105.Gary Delorme-4(Elise Marie Rollande Guillet-3, Louis Guillet-2, Francois Guillet-1) was born on 11 Jun 1949 in Prince Albert, SK. He married Gail Kennedy on 01 Mar 1980 in Prince Albert SK. She was born on 22 Apr 1955 in Prince Albert, SK. He married Iris Dianne Iverson on 13 May 1972.

Children of Gary Delorme and Gail Kennedy are:
    i.   Jeff Delorme, B: 28 Aug 1982 in Prince Albert, SK.
    ii.   Christopher Delorme, B: 21 Sep 1988 in Prince Albert, SK.
    iii.   Kelly Delorme, B: 01 Sep 1991 in Prince Albert, SK.

106.John Delorme-4(Elise Marie Rollande Guillet-3, Louis Guillet-2, Francois Guillet-1) was born on 12 Dec 1952 in Prince Albert, SK. He married Judy Laird on 01 May 1971 in Prince Albert, SK. She was born on 22 Oct 1952.

Children of John Delorme and Judy Laird are:
  i.   Michael Delorme, B: 06 Nov 1971.
  ii. Laurie Delorme, B: 20 Feb 1974.

107. Linda Kustaski-4(Laura Ethier-3, Camille Guillet-2, Francois Guillet-1). She married Rene Detillieux.

Children of Linda Kustaski and Rene Detillieux are:
  i.   Chantelle Detillieux.
  ii. Wendy Detillieux.

108.Vern Kustaski-4(Laura Ethier-3, Camille Guillet-2, Francois Guillet-1). He married Jeanne Theoret.

Child of Vern Kustaski and Jeanne Theoret is:
  i.   Jordan Kustaski.

109. Elaine Kustaski-4(Laura Ethier-3, Camille Guillet-2, Francois Guillet-1). She married Stephan Hrapchak.

Children of Elaine Kustaski and Stephan Hrapchak are:
  i.   Wes Hrapchak.
  ii. Les Hrapchak.
  iii. Kimberly Hrapchak.

110. Robert Kustaski-4(Laura Ethier-3, Camille Guillet-2, Francois Guillet-1). He married Carol Hnidy.

Child of Robert Kustaski and Carol Hnidy is:
  i.   Laurisa Kustaski.

GENERATION 5

111. Nicole Haw-5(Sharyn Edith Dianne Guillet-4, Edward Guillet-3, Henri Francois Guillet-2, Francois Guillet-1) was born on 02 May 1970 in Dawson Creek, BC. She married Cerise Irving in Chetwynd, BC. She married Kevin Browne in Chetwynd, BC. Now divorced.

> Child of Nicole Haw and Cerise Irving is:
> i.   Chelsie Irving Browne, B: 01 Nov 1991 in Chetwynd, BC.

> Children of Nicole Haw and Kevin Browne are:
> i.   Hunter Browne, B: 28 May 1998 in Chetwynd, BC.
> ii. Sierra Browne, B: 10 Sep 1996 in Chetwynd, BC.

112. Connie-Jo Haw-5(Sharyn Edith Dianne Guillet-4, Edward Guillet-3, Henri Francois Guillet-2, Francois Guillet-1) was born on 13 Jul 1977 in Chetwynd, BC. She met Brian Gallant.

> Child of Connie Jo Haw and Brian Gallant is:
> i.   Ebanie Savanah Gallant, B: 14 Dec 1994 in Dawson Creek, BC.

> Child of Connie-Jo Haw and Jeffery Franklin is:
> i.   Ayvarie Samantha Franklin, B: 19 Apr 1999 in Chetwynd, BC.

> Child of Connie-Jo Haw and Keith William Maisey is:
> i.   Loula Sophia Maisey, B: 09 Oct 2007 in Dawson Creek, BC.

113. Tammy Lynne Guillet-5(Dennis Edward Norman Guillet-4, Edward Guillet-3, Henri Francois Guillet-2, Francois is Guillet-1) was born on 28 Mar 1969 in Dawson Creek, BC. She married Arnold Szelecz. She married James Melvin Schonwald on 26 Oct 1990 in Medicine Hat, AB.

> Child of Tammy Lynne Guillet and Arnold Szelecz is:
> i.   Dennis Joseph Szelecz, B: 22 Jul 1999 in Kamloops, BC.

Children of Tammy Lynne Guillet and James Melvin Schonwald are:
  i. Megan Mary-Lynn Schonwald, B: 21 Jan 1991 in Fort St. John, BC.
  ii. Rialey-Ann Paige Schonwald, B: 31 Aug 1992 in Fort St. John, BC.
  iii. Braidon Kenden Schonwald, B: 14 Dec 1995 in Fort St. John, BC.

114. Theresa Simone Guillet-5(Dennis Edward Norman Guillet-4, Edward Guillet-3, Henri Francois Guillet-2, Francois Guillet-1) was born on 26 Nov 1971 in Chetwynd, BC. She married Curtis Rubin Lizotte on 02 Sep 1995 in Taylor, BC.

Children of Theresa Simone Guillet and Curtis Rubin Lizotte are:
  i. Kristen Emily Lizotte, B: 17 Feb 1995 in Fort St. John, BC.
  ii. Erin Simone Lizotte, B: 14 Apr 1996 in Fort St. John, BC.
  iii. Jenna Marie Lizotte, B: 31 Oct 1997 in Fort St. John, BC.

115. Candice Gail Guillet-5(Ernest Henry Guillet-4, Edward Guillet-3, Henri Francois Guillet-2, Francois Guillet-1) was born on 06 Jul 1985 in Chetwynd, BC. She married Kevin McLaren on Jul 2005 in Chetwynd, BC.

Child of Candice Gail Guillet and Kevin McLaren is:
  i. Reese William McLaren, B: 07 Oct 2006 in Grande Prairie, AB.

116. Lisa Marie Guillet-5(Ernest Henry Guillet-4, Edward Guillet-3, Henri Francois Guillet-2, Francois Guillet-1) was born on 06 Feb 1968 in Dawson Creek, BC. She married Jim Smith. She married Bryan Breault on 17 Sep 1994.

Child of Lisa Marie Guillet and Jim Smith is:
  i. Colbie James Smith, B: 31 Oct 1986 in Dawson Creek, BC.

117.Bridget Jeanette Guillet-5(Donald Lorne Guillet-4, Edward Guillet-3, Henri Francois Guillet-2, Francois Guillet-1) was born on 06 Sep 1967 in Dawson Creek, BC. She married John William Kolosky on 20 Jul 1985 in Chetwynd, BC. He was born on 10 Nov 1960 in Grande Prairie, AB. She married Fredrick Ivan Steen on 14 Jul 2001 in Chetwynd, BC, son of Joseph Paul Steen and Madeline Alec. He was born on 27 Jul 1968 in Dawson Creek, BC.

Children of Bridget Jeanette Guillet and John William Kolosky are:
  i.   Jeris John Kolosky, B: 14 Sep 1986 in Chetwynd, BC.
       D: 21 May 2010, Chetwynd, BC.
  ii. Jamie Donald Kolosky, B: 06 Apr 1988 in Dawson Creek, BC.

Child of Bridget Jeanette Guillet and Fredrick Ivan Steen is:
  i.   Presley Sharlene Steen, B: 08 Sep 2000 in Prince George, BC.

128.Dawn Lee Guillet-5(Donald Lorne Guillet-4, Edward Guillet-3, Henri Francois Guillet-2, Francois Guillet-1) was born on 14 Oct 1971 in Chetwynd, BC. She married Daniel Will Jolin Jr. on 11 Nov 1994 in Chetwynd, BC.

Children of Dawn Lee Guillet and Daniel Will Jolin Jr. are:
  157.Coltin Jolin, B: 17 Dec 1992 in Chetwynd, BC.
  158.Quinton Jolin, B: 14 Aug 1994 in Chetwynd, BC.

129.Maxime Edward Leslie Guillet-5(Leslie Gordon Guillet-4, Edward Guillet-3, Henri Francois Guillet-2, Francois Guillet-1) was born on 25 Aug 1974 in Edmonton, AB. He married Deanne Heather Cheesman on 12 Jun 2002 in Harrison Hot Springs, BC, daughter of Kenneth Harry Cheesman and Helen Elaine Mueller. She was born on 09 May 1974 in Fort St. John, BC.

Children of Maxime Edward Leslie Guillet and Deanne Heather Cheesman are:
  157. Laurana Nicole Guillet, B: 22 Nov 2005 in Abbotsford, BC.
  158. Kieriana Alyssa Guillet, B: 30 Dec 2007 in Abbotsford, BC.

130. Michael Gordon Jerald Guillet-5(Leslie Gordon Guillet-4, Edward Guillet-3, Henri Francois Guillet-2, Francois Guillet-1) was born on 25 Sep 1977 in Fort St. John, BC. He married Lisa Marie Cardinal.

Child of Michael Gordon Jerald Guillet and Lisa Marie Cardinal is:
  i.   Steven Leslie Guillet, B: 16 Jul 2001 in Fort St. John, BC.

Child of Michael Gordon Jerald Guillet and Jennifer Mae Hale is:
  i.   Boston Rain Guillet, B: 13 Sep 2005 in Edmonton, AB.

121. Collin Rene Guillet-5(Norman Daryl Guillet-4, Edward Guillet-3, Henri Francois Guillet-2, Francois Guillet-1) was born on 27 Feb 1980 in Chetwynd, BC. He married Becky-Jo Hagerman, daughter of Richard Hagerman and Debora Ann Butcher. She was born on 22 Jun 1980 in Frederickton, NB.

Child of Collin Rene Guillet and Becky-Jo Hagerman is:
  i.   Brailee Rae Guillet, B: 14 Jul 2003 in Chetwynd, BC.

122. Loni James Shevkenek-5(Sandra Lynn Guillet-4, Edward Guillet-3, Henri Francois Guillet-2, Francois Guillet-1) was born on 22 Mar 1977 in Chetwynd, BC. He married Natalie Keizer, daughter of Grayson Keizer and Velma Rogers. She was born on 09 Jun 1977 in Kentville, NS.

Children of Loni James Shevkenek and Natalie Keizer are:
  i.   Kennedy Adele Shevkenek, B: 21 Jun 2004 in Dawson Creek, BC.
  ii. Sheldon Grayson James Shevkenek, B: 09 Aug 2006 in Dawson Creek, BC.

123. Trudy Lynn Shevkenek-5(Sandra Lynn Guillet-4, Edward Guillet-3, Henri Francois Guillet-2, Francois Guillet-1) was born on 30 Aug 1978 in Fort St. John BC. She married Trevor Ducharme, son of Ronald Ducharme and Lorraine McAvany. He was born on 24 Sep 1980 in Chetwynd, BC.

Children of Trudy Lynn Shevkenek and Trevor Ducharme are:
    i.   Talia Lynn-Marie Ducharme, B: 29 May 1998 in Fort St. John, BC.
    ii.   Trinity Emily Ducharme, B: 31 Dec 2000 in Grande Prairie, AB.
    iii. Teagan Emily Marie Ducharme, B: 15 Aug 2005 in Prince George, BC.

124. Gerald Paul Comeau-5(Anita Marie Cecile Ethier-4, Henriette Guillet-3, Henri Francois Guillet-2, Francois Guillet-1) was born on 24 Oct 1954 in Peace River, AB. He married Theresa Nesdoly on 14 Jul 1984 in Edmonton, AB. She was born on 05 Apr 1965.

Children of Gerald Paul Comeau and Theresa Nesdoly are:
    i.   Robyn Lyne Comeau, B: 25 May 1987.
    ii.   Sarah Comeau, B: 29 Jan 1992.

125. Richard Louise Comeau-5(Anita Marie Cecile Ethier-4, Henriette Guillet-3, Henri Francois Guillet-2, Francois Guillet-1) was born on 31 Aug 1955 in Peace River, AB. He married Marie Coons on 03 Nov 1973 in Peace River, BC. She was born on 08 Feb 1958 in Vancouver, BC. He married Doris Audet on 27 Apr 1985. She was born on 11 Apr 1965.

Children of Richard Louise Comeau and Marie Coons are:
153. i.   Tina Marie Gail Comeau, B: 06 Jun 1974 in Prince Albert, SK.
      ii.   Jason Lee Comeau, B: 05 Jun 1975 in St. Albert, AB.
154. iii. Renee Comeau, B: 02 Apr 1978 in Edmonton, AB.
      iv. Christal Comeau, B: 08 Feb 1980 in Edmonton, AB.

Child of Richard Louise Comeau and Doris Audet is:
    i.   Paul Comeau, B: 25 Oct 1986.

126.Victor Phillip Comeau-5(Anita Marie Cecile Ethier-4, Henriette Guillet-3, Henri Francois Guillet-2, Francois Guillet-1) was born on 09 Aug 1956 in Peace River, AB. He married Shelda Ann Coons on 02 Aug 1975 in Peace River, BC. She was born on 20 Jan 1959 in Vancouver, BC.

Children of Victor Phillip Comeau and Shelda Ann Coons are:
155. i. Nicole Lynn Comeau, B: 14 Sept 1976 in Fort McMurray, AB, M: 30 Sept 2000.
ii. Marcel Victor Comeau, B: 26 May 1978 in Fort McMurray, AB.
iii. Brittany Marie Comeau, B: 14 Dec 1987.
iv. Stephanie Gail Comeau, B: 09 Feb 1989.

127. Denise Raymond Comeau-5(Anita Marie Cecile Ethier-4, Henriette Guillet-3, Henri Francois Guillet-2, Francois Guillet-1) was born on 17 Nov 1957 in Peace River, AB. He married Kimberley Cameron on 20 Mar 1982. She was born on 12 Jun 1958, Alberta Canada.

Children of Denise Raymond Comeau and Kimberley Cameron are:
i. Shawna Comeau, B: 24 Oct 1983.

Children of Denise Raymond Comeau and Karen Coons are:
156. i. Jennifer Gail Comeau, B: 20 Aug 1974 in St. Albert, AB, M: 20 May 1995.
ii. Shelda Anne Comeau, B: 24 Nov 1975 in Edmonton, AB.

128.Claude Eugene Comeau-5(Anita Marie Cecile Ethier-4, Henriette Guillet-3, Henri Francois Guillet-2, Francois Guillet-1) was born on 26 Jan 1959 in Fort St. John, BC. He died on 15 May 1981 in High Prairie, AB. He married Kimberley Cameron. She was born on 12 Jun 1958, Alberta Canada.

Child of Claude Eugene Comeau and Kimberley Cameron is:
i. Lisa Michelle Comeau, B: 15 Jul 1981 in Edmonton, AB, M: 23 Oct 2004.

129.Claudette Marie Dianne Comeau-5(Anita Marie Cecile Ethier-4, Henriette Guillet-3, Henri Francois Guillet-2, Francois Guillet-1) was born on 28 Apr 1960 in Peace River, AB. She died on 29 Oct 1998 in Peace River, AB. She married Larry Wielgosz on 21 Oct 1978 in Rose Valley, SK, son of Nick Wielgosz and Anne Wielgosz. He was born on 13 Apr 1957 in Rose Valley, SK. He died on 03 Sep 2000 in Golden, BC. She married Gregg Foss on 27 Jun 1992. He was born on 06 May 1956.

Children of Claudette Marie Dianne Comeau and Larry Wielgosz are:
157. i.   Mark Wielgosz, B: 25 Oct 1979 in Edmonton, AB, M: 07 Oct 1999.
      ii. Eric Wielgosz, B: 20 Jun 1981 in Edmonton, AB.

130.Roger Comeau-5(Anita Marie Cecile Ethier-4, Henriette Guillet-3, Henri Francois Guillet-2, Francois Guillet-1) was born on 14 Jan 1963. He married Barbara Plamondon.

Children of Roger Comeau and Barbara Plamondon are:
      i.   Carrie Anne Comeau, B: 13 Apr 1983.
      ii. Carly Joan Comeau, B: 23 Mar 1988.

131.Michael Patrick Comeau-5(Anita Marie Cecile Ethier-4, Henriette Guillet-3, Henri Francois Guillet-2, Francois Guillet-1) was born on 03 Jul 1964 in Peace River, AB. He married Maureen Schneider on 23 May 1987. She was born on 19 Apr 1964.

Children of Michael Patrick Comeau and Maureen Schneider are:
      i.   Kristopher Schneider Comeau, B: 09 Sep 1981.
      ii. Angela Marie Comeau, B: 21 Dec 1987.
      iii. Sean Claude Comeau, B: 03 Jun 1989.

132. Brian Edward Ethier-5(Edouard Charles Maurice Ethier-4, Henriette Guillet-3, Henri Francois Guillet-2, Francois Guillet-1) was born on 03 Mar 1970 in Dawson Creek, BC. He married Antonieta Martins on 23 Aug 1997 in Chetwynd, BC. She was born on 05 Apr 1972 in Chetwynd, BC.

Children of Brian Edward Ethier and Antonieta Martins are:
    i.   Dylan Martins Ethier, B: 09 Sep 2002.
    ii.   Scott Martins Ethier, B: 10 Feb 2008.

133. Patricia Anne Podolecki-5(Denise Marie Ethier-4, Henriette Guillet-3, Henri Francois Guillet-2, Francois Guillet-1) was born on 03 May 1962 in Dawson Creek, BC. She married Stewart Cameron on 09 Feb 1985 in Chetwynd, BC. He was born on 05 Sep 1955 in Dawson Creek, BC.

Children of Patricia Anne Podolecki and Stewart Cameron are:
    i.   Brandon Lance Cameron, B: 28 Sep 1981 in Prince George, BC.
    ii.   Janelle Dene Cameron, B: 09 Oct 1984 in Fort St. John, BC.
    iii.   Donavan Trent Cameron, B: 13 Feb 1986 in Kelowna, BC.
    iv.   Quaid Stewart Cameron, B: 07 Oct 1988 in Kelowna, BC.
    v.   Shalayne Patrict Mary-Ann Cameron, B: 01 Nov 1991 in Kelowna, BC.

134. Michael Peter Podolecki-5(Denise Marie Ethier-4, Henriette Guillet-3, Henri Francois Guillet-2, Francois Guillet-1) was born on 01 Apr 1963 in Williams Lake B.C. He married Elaine Wallace on 02 Jul 1988 in Chetwynd BC. She was born on 16 Jun 1968 in Dawson Creek, BC. He married Leann Wheeler 21 May 2005. She was born on 25 Sep 1966 in Prince Rupert, BC.

Children of Michael Peter Podolecki and Elaine Wallace are:
    i.   Stephen Podolecki, B: 25 May 1991 in Dawson Creek, BC.
    ii.   Jenna Podolecki, B: 08 Jun 1993 in Dawson Creek, BC.

Richard Matthew Podolecki, 5(Denise Marie Ethier-4, Henriette Guillet-3, Henri Francois Guillet-2, Francois Guillet-1) was born on 06 Jun 1964 in Williams Lake, BC. M: Norma Gauthier.

135. Colin James Wittstruck-5(Aline Marie Ethier-4, Henriette Guillet-3, Henri Francois Guillet-2, Francois Guillet-1) was born on 20 Aug 1973 in Fort St. John, BC. He married Wendy (Unknown) on 15 Jul 1995.

Child of Colin James Wittstruck and Wendy (Unknown) is:
    i.   Vanessa Laurea Wittstruck, B: 13 Dec 1997 in Prince George, BC.

136. Connie Lee Ethier-5(Leonard Ronald Ethier-4, Alice Gabrielle Guillet-3, Henri Francois Guillet-2, Francois Guillet-1) was born on 17 Nov 1965 in Sudbury, ON. She married Shawn Hynes.

Child of Connie Lee Ethier and Shawn Hynes is:
    i.   Rylee Lee Hynes, B: 15 Jun 1988 in Sudbury, ON.

137. Lisa Prefontaine-5(Daniel Prefontaine-4, Gabrielle Guillet-3, Henri Francois Guillet-2, Francois Guillet-1) was born on 15 Dec 1965 in Prince Albert, SK. She married Grant Dott on 18 Aug 1995 in Ottawa, ON. He was born on 28 Dec 1964 in Dundee, Scotland.

Child of Lisa Prefontaine and Grant Dott is:
    i.   Callum Charles Dott, B: 02 Sep 1996 in Portland, OR, USA.

138. Dale Lestage-5(Augustine Sarrasin-4, Agnes Guillet-3, Eugene Leon Guillet-2, Francois Guillet-1) was born on 20 Jun 1962. He married Dainne (Unknown).

Child of Dale Lestage and Dainne (Unknown) is:
    i.   Arron Michal Lestage, B: 11 Jun 1991.

139. Deanna Lestage-5(Augustine Sarrasin-4 Agnes Guillet-3, Eugene Leon Guillet-2, Francois Guillet-1) was born on 15 Aug 1960. She married Roy Ferguson.

Gary, Deanna, Greg
Jazlyn and Keith

Children of Deanna Lestage and Roy Ferguson are:
    i.   Gary Ferguson.
   ii.   Greg Ferguson.

140. David Lestage-5(Augustine Sarrasin-4, Agnes Guillet-3, Eugene Leon Guillet-2, Francois Guillet-1) was born on 03 Oct 1963. He married Tammy (Unknown).

Child of David Lestage and Tammy (Unknown) is:
    i.   Cole Lestage.

141. Laurie Ann Ferguson-5(Marie Sarrasin-4, Agnes Guillet-3, Eugene Leon Guillet-2, Francois Guillet-1).

    i.   Cassandra Marie Ferguson, B: 03 Feb 1991.

142. Scott Ferguson-5(Marie Sarrasin-4, Agnes Guillet-3, Eugene Leon Guillet-2, Francois Guillet-1) was born in 1969. He married Sheila (Unknown).

Child of Scott Ferguson and Sheila (Unknown) is:
    i.   Christopher Scott Ferguson, B: 17 Aug 1991.

143. Jessica Dumont-5(Roger Jules Eugene Dumont-4, Irene Guillet-3, Eugene Leon Guillet-2, Francois Guillet-1) was born on 28 Jan 1977 in Regina, SK. She married Reid Besden on 12 Aug 2000 in Regina, SK.

Child of Jessica Dumont and Reid Besden is:
    i.   Keane Besden, B: 15 Dec 1994.

144. Michele Dumont-5(Denis Arestride Dumont-4, Irene Guillet-3, Eugene Leon Guillet-2, Francois Guillet-1) was born on 09 Dec 1974. She married John Miller on 13 Aug in Regina, SK. He was born on 30 Nov 1972.

Children of Michele Dumont and John Miller are:
  i.   Dilon Miller, B: 05 Jun 1995.
  ii. Anthony Miller, B: 14 Sep 1998.

145. Donna Clark-5(Darlene Guillet-4, Leon Guillet-3, Eugene Leon Guillet-2, Francois Guillet-1) was born on 16 Sept 1975.

Children of Donna Clark are:
  i.   Stephanie Clark. B: 21 Jan 1994
  ii. Keiran Clark. B: 16 Apr 2001

Keiran Clark, Donna Clark and Darlene Pounder

146. William Clark-5(Darlene Guillet-4, Leon Guillet-3, Eugene Leon Guillet-2, Francois Guillet-1). B: 21 July 1974.

Child of William Clark is:
  i.   Brandon Clark. B: 21 Feb 1997

William Clark and son Brandon

147. Cindy Darlene Guillet-5(Lawrence Guillet-4, Leon Guillet-3, Eugene Leon Guillet-2, Francois Guillet-1) was born on 17 Aug 1978 in Vancouver, BC. She married Lance Christie on 01 Apr 2006 in Edmonton, AB. He was born on 01 Apr 1976 in Ontario.

Children of Cindy Darlene Guillet and Lance Christie are:
  i.   Grace Christie, B: 26 Jun 2003.
  ii. Amber Christie, B: 13 Feb 2007 in Edmonton, AB.

148.Angeline Petz-5(Claudette Lorette Lestage-4, Aline Guillet-3, Eugene Leon Guillet-2, Francois Guillet-1) was born on 02 Feb 1976. She married Kelly Nathan Klassen. He was born on 13 Jun 1975.

Children of Angeline Petz and Kelly Nathan Klassen are:
   i.   Rayelle Klassen, B: 04 Feb 2000.
   ii. Joryn Klassen, B: 08 Aug 1997.

149. Derek Petz-5(Claudette Lorette Lestage-4, Aline Guillet-3, Eugene Leon Guillet-2, Francois Guillet-1) was born on 13 Dec 1979. He married Kristin Reslein. She was born on 23 Feb 1979.

Child of Derek Petz and Kristin Reslein is:
   i.   Kaleb Petz, B: 31 Mar 2002.

150. Steven Fredrick Denness-5(Belinda Ann Guillet-4, Raymond Albert Guillet-3, Eugene Leon Guillet-2, Francois Guillet-1) was born on 09 Jan 1981 in Vancouver, BC. He met Crystal Littlejohn, daughter of Glenn Littlejohn and Wonda Mcdonald. She was born on 12 Jun 1983 in Prince George, BC.

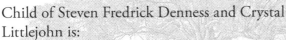

Steven Denness, Crystal Littlejohn and son Austin

Child of Steven Fredrick Denness and Crystal Littlejohn is:
   i.   Austin Emerson Denness, B: 29 Jun 2004 in Surrey Memorial Hospital at 2:30pm.

Austin Denness

151. Tanya Ann Davidson-5(Ramona Marie Guillet-4, Raymond Albert Guillet-3, Eugene Leon Guillet-2, Francois Guillet-1) was born on 28 Sep 1982 in Kamloops, BC. She married Richard Mason on 02 Aug 2003 in Chetwynd, BC, son of Richard Mason Sr. and Leona Ducharme. He was born on 07 Dec 1975 in Williams Lake, BC. He died on 19 May 2005 in Chetwynd, BC.

Tanya and Krista

Richard Mason and Krista Mason

She married Clayton Doll on 26 Jul 2008 in Dawson Creek, BC, son of Wayne Doll and Katherine. He was born on 03 Feb 1983 in Kitwanga, BC.

Tanya and Clayton Doll 2008

Child of Tanya Ann Davidson and Richard Mason is:
  i.   Krista Marie Mason, B: 05 Dec 2001 in Dawson Creek, BC.

152. Jamie Lynn Davidson5(Ramona Marie Guillet-4, Raymond Albert Guillet-3, Eugene Leon Guillet-2, Francois Guillet-1) was born on 03 Jun 1984 in Kamloops, BC. She married Michael Collins on 03 Jul, 2010 in Chetwynd, BC, son of Daniel James Sheman Collins and Hazel Ross. He was born on 29 Aug 1977 in Chetwynd, BC.

Jamie (Davidson) and Mike Collins

Alyshia, Jamie and Lindsey

Children of Jamie Lynn Davidson and Michael Collins are:
  i. Alyshia Leona Collins, B: 21 Oct 2003 in Dawson Creek, BC.
 ii. Lindsey Michelle Collins, B: 06 Jul 2007 in Dawson Creek, BC.

GENERATION 6

153. Tina Marie Gail Comeau-6(Richard Louise Comeau-5, Anita Marie Cecile Ethier-4, Henriette Guillet-3, Henri Francois Guillet-2, Francois Guillet-1) was born on 06 Jun 1974 in Prince Albert, SK. She married Aaron Matheson.

Children of Tina Marie Gail Comeau and Aaron Matheson are:
i. Brandon Lee Matheson, B: 13 Jan 1993.
ii. Braydon Matheson, B: 24 Aug 1996.
iii. Jordan Matheson, B: 18 Jun 1999.

154. Renee Comeau-6(Richard Louise Comeau-5, Anita Marie Cecile Ethier-4, Henriette Guillet-3, Henri Francois Guillet-2, Francois Guillet-1) was born on 02 Apr 1978 in Edmonton, AB. She met Randy Kolody.

Children of Renee Comeau and Randy Kolody are:
i. Kristen Kolody, B: 07 Dec 1997.
ii. Joshua Kolody, B: 27 Oct 1999.
iii. Brice Kolody, B: 16 Jun 2001.
iv. Hanna Kolody, B: 14 Dec 2002.

155. Nicole Lynn Comeau-6(Victor Phillip Comeau-5, Anita Marie Cecile Ethier-4, Henriette Guillet-3, Henri Francois Guillet-2, Francois Guillet-1) was born on 14 Sep 1976 in Fort McMurray, AB. She married Ian McFatridge on 30 Sep 2000. He was born on 10 May 1976.

Children of Nicole Lynn Comeau and Ian McFatridge are:
i. Dylan McFatridge, B: 10 Jul 2002.
ii. Jayce McFatridge, B: 30 Nov 2004.

156. Jennifer Gail Comeau-6(Denise Raymond Comeau-5, Anita Marie Cecile Ethier-4, Henriette Guillet-3, Henri Francois Guillet-2, Francois Guillet-1) was born on 20 Aug 1974 in St. Albert, AB. She married Gabe Gattacea on 20 May 1995.

Children of Jennifer Gail Comeau and Gabe Gattacea are:
    i.   Kristen Gail Gattacea, B: 10 Mar 1997.
   ii.   Daniel Vincent Gattacea, B: 11 Mar 1998.

157. Mark Wielgosz-6(Claudette Marie Dianne Comeau-5, Anita Marie Cecile Ethier-4, Henriette Guillet-3, Henri Francois Guillet-2, Francois Guillet-1) was born on 25 Oct 1979 in Edmonton, AB. He married Cassandra Whiting on 07 Oct 1999. She was born on 18 Dec 1979.

Children of Mark Wielgosz and Cassandra Whiting are:
    i.   Taylin Wielgosz, B: 04 Jun 2001.
   ii.   Landen Cole Wielgosz, B: 30 Aug 2003.

EUGENE LEON GUILLET MEMORIAL

GUILLET – Eugene Leon, husband of Mrs. Angeline Guillet of 220 - 10th Street East passed away in local hospital in his 72ed year. Prayer service will be held in the MacKenzie Chapel on Sunday, May 8th at 8 p.m. Rt. Rev. Msgr. J. A. Boucher will celebrate Requiem High Mass in the Sacred Heart Cathedral on Monday, May 9th at 10 a.m. Internment in the family plot at Memorial Gardens. Besides his wife, Mr. Guillet is survived by five sons, Gilbert of Domremy, John of Regina, Leo and Raymond of Vancouver and Paul at home and four daughters; Mrs. Albert (Agnes) Sarrazin of 220 - 10th Street East, Mrs. Paul (Fraces) Hamel, Mrs. Leo (Irene) Dumont and Mrs. Albert (Aline) Lestage, all of Regina, 40 grandchildren and six great grandchildren, two sisters; Mrs. M. Baribeau of Edmonton and Mrs. C. Ethier of Domremy, one brother Henri of Domremy. The late Mr. Guillet was a Vetern of World War One. Born in France and came to Prince Albert in 1896. Farmed at Domremy until his retirement to Prince Albert in 1950. Arrangements by MacKenzie Funeral Home.

ANGELINE
(PILON) GUILLET
MEMORIAL

GUILLET - Angeline, passed away peacefully after a brief illness at Pioneer Village in Regina on Tuesday, September 23, 1997. Born December 8, 1900 in Batoche, North West Territories, she was the oldest daughter of Joseph Pilon and Juliana Braconnier. Shortly after World War I she moved to Domremy, Saskatchewan, where she was employed as a domestic worker by the family of her future husband. She married Eugene Guillet in 1920 and settled on his homestead in Domremy where they lived until moving to Prince Albert in 1951. In 1970 a few years after the sudden death of her husband Mrs. Guillet moved to Regina and lived with her youngest son Paul until 1991. Predeceased by her husband in 1966, Mrs. Guillet is survived by nine children; four daughters; Agnes Sarrasin of Prince Albert, Francis Hamel, Irene Dumont and Aline Lestage all from Regina; and five sons; Gilbert from Prince Albert, Leo in Kamloops, B.C., Raymond in Grande Prairie, Alta.; and John and Paul in Regina. Mrs. Guillet is also survived by forty-one grandchildren, seventy-six great-grandchildren, twenty-five great, great grandchildren and one great, great, great granddaughter. A Prayer Service will be held at the Regina Funeral Home, Hwy #1 East, on Thursday, September 25, 1997 at 8:00 p.m. A Requiem High Mass will be celebrated at the Sacred Heart Cathedral, 1401 4th Ave, West, in Prince Albert on Friday, September 26, 1997 at 3:00 p.m. Interment will follow at the Prince Albert Memorial Gardens. In lieu of flowers, donations can be made in Mrs. Guillet's name to any benevolent or charitable organizations. Arrangements are in care of the REGINA FUNERAL HOME (Phone 789-8850).

EUGENE GUILLET AND BOYS

Raymond, Gilbert, Eugene, Johnny, Leo

EUGENE GUILLET FAMILY PHOTOS

(back) Paul, Leo, Aline, Gilbert, Johnny, Raymond, Irene
(front) Agnes, Angeline, Frances

(back) Johnny, Leo, Raymond, Gilbert
(front) Frances, Aline, Irene, Agnes

EDWARD GUILLET FAMILY PHOTOS

Norman, Kevin, Dennis, Donny
Laurelle, Sharyn, Leslie, Jeanette
Edward and Irene

Becky, Collin, Brandy
Connie, Don and Brailee

91

ALINE (GUILLET) LESTAGE
FAMILY PHOTOS

*Gary, Roland,
Greg, Rodney and Claudette*

*Aline, Albert, Claudette
Gary, Roland, Valerie, Greg and Rodney*

Valerie

GREGORY LESTAGE MEMORIAL

LESTAGE – October 25, 1977, Gregory Leslie Lestage, beloved son of Albert and Aline and late of 973 Queen St. passed away at age 18 years. Besides his parents, Gregory is survived by three brothers, Roland, Gary, and Rodney all of Regina, and two sisters Claudette and Valerie also of Regina and two Grandmothers Mrs. Angeline Guillet, Regina and Mrs. Yvonne Lestage, Kamloops, B.C. Funeral mass on Saturday October 29 at 10 a.m. in Sacred Heart R.C. Church with Fr. J. Balzer the celebrant. Internment Regina Memorial Gardens. Prayers on Friday Oct. 28 at 8 p.m. in the chapel of the Lee Funeral Home. Arrangements in care of Lee Funeral Home. Regina and Cupar, John Lipp funeral Director.

Darlene (Guillet) Pounder wedding family photo

Leo Guillet

Cathy Guillet

MARY GUILLET MEMORIAL

Housewife rites held on Tuesday

Funeral rites for the late Mrs. Mary Guillet, 7628 - 202A St., Langley, were held on Tuesday morning, March 24th at ten o'clock in St. Joseph's Roman Catholic Church in Langley City. Rev. Father J. Comey officiated and arrangements were directed by Henderson's Langley Funeral Home. Cremation was in Victory Memorial Park crematorium in Surrey.

Mrs. Guillet, 51, suc-cumbed in Langley Memorial Hospital on Friday last week, March 20th. She was born in Regina, Sask., on December 11th, 1929, and moved from Regina to Vancouver 25 years ago. For the past six years she had been a resident at her late address in Langley.

Family surviving Mrs. Guillet's death are: her husband, Leo; four daughters, Mrs. W. (Darlene) Clark, Cassiar, B.C., Irene in Vancouver, Cathy and Sharon both at home; a son, Lawrence, in Langley; and three grandchildren.

RAYMOND GUILLET FAMILY PHOTOS

Raymond

Leona and Eugene

Ramona, Belinda and Leona

Elaina and Ramona

EUGENE (JR) GUILLET MEMORIAL

GUILLET – Eugene Raymond (Butch), peacefully at his residence, September 6, 1989 age 32 years. He will be lovingly remembered by his family, his loving wife, Ingrid; one son, Corey; mother and father, Raymond and Annette; three sisters, Belinda, Ramona, and Elaina. Butch, as he was well known by, is also survived by his father and mother-in-law, Ernest and Maria Abolis; a host of friends, relatives, and his dearest friends Jim and Sylvia Mennear. Butch was predeceased by his sister, Leona in 1965. Prayers will be said on Monday, September 11 at 8 p.m. from the Immaculate Conception Roman Catholic Church, 8842 119 Street, Delta. Mass of Christian Burial will be celebrated September 12 at 10 a.m. by Reverend Don Larson. Internment will follow in Valley View Memorial Garden. Flowers will be greatfully accepted, although donations to the B.C. Cancer Society would be appreciated.

VALLEY VIEW 596-8866

KINSHIP REPORT FOR FRANCOIS GUILLET

Name:	Birth Date:	Relationship:
(Unknown), Wendy		2nd Great Granddaughter-In-Law
Abolis, Ingrid		Great Granddaughter-In-Law
Arne, Bonnie Marie	2-Dec-76	2nd Great Granddaughter
Arne, Dean	3-Oct-71	2nd Great Grandson
Audet, Doris	11-Apr-65	2nd Great Granddaughter-In-Law
Baribeau, Alida	1907	Granddaughter
Baribeau, Beatrice		Great Granddaughter
Baribeau, Bruno	12-Mar-1883	Son-In-Law
Baribeau, Denise	1916	Granddaughter
Baribeau, George	1906	Grandson
Baribeau, Helene	1909	Granddaughter
Baribeau, Irene	1914	Granddaughter
Baribeau, Jacqueline		Great Granddaughter
Baribeau, Laure	1915	Granddaughter
Baribeau, Loretta		Great Granddaughter
Baribeau, Lorraine		Great Granddaughter
Baribeau, Lucien	1905	Grandson
Baribeau, Raymond		Great Grandson
Baribeau, Yvonne		Great Granddaughter
Bastide, Ernest		Grandson-In-Law
Bastide, Ernie		Great Grandson
Bastide, Louise		Great Granddaughter
Bastide, Maurice		Great Granddaughter
Bastide, Raymond		Great Grandson
Batt, Neil		2nd Great Grandson-In-Law
Beamish, Lorrie Ann		Great Granddaughter-In-Law
Beattie, Richard	25-Sep-59	Great Grandson-In-Law
Beaudry, Brian	2-Mar-46	Great Grandson-In-Law
Beaudry, Brian Scott	23-Mar-67	2nd Great Grandson
Besden, Keane	15-Dec-94	3rd Great Grandson
Besden, Reid		2nd Great Grandson-In-Law
Bibaud, Winnifred	6-Apr-54	Great Granddaughter-In-Law
Billo, Arsene Emile		Great Grandson-In-Law
Billo, Devon	6-Jul-76	2nd Great Grandson

Billo, Kachelle	28-Mar-86	2nd Great Granddaughter
Billo, Keith	31-Aug-73	2nd Great Grandson
Blackstock		Grandson-In-Law
Blackstock, Berna		Great Granddaughter
Blandford, Charlene		2nd Great Granddaughter-In-Law
Boutin, Jille		Great Grandson-In-Law
Breault, Bryan		2nd Great Grandson-In-Law
Browne, Chelsie Irving	1-Nov-91	3rd Great Granddaughter
Browne, Hunter	28-May-98	3rd Great Granddaughter
Browne, Kevin		2nd Great Grandson-In-Law
Browne, Sierra	10-Sep-96	3rd Great Granddaughter
Bymoen, Crystal		2nd Great Granddaughter-In-Law
Cameron, Brandon Lance	28-Sep-81	3rd Great Grandson
Cameron, Donavan Trent	13-Feb-86	3rd Great Grandson
Cameron, Janelle Dene	9-Oct-84	3rd Great Granddaughter
Cameron, Ken	9-Jun-47	Great Grandson-In-Law
Cameron, Kimberley	12-Jun-58	2nd Great Granddaughter-In-Law
Cameron, Quaid Stewart	7-Oct-88	3rd Great Grandson
Cameron, Shalayne Patrica Mary-Ann	1-Nov-91	3rd Great Granddaughter
Cameron, Stewart	5-Sep-55	2nd Great Grandson-In-Law
Cardinal, Lisa Marie		2nd Great Granddaughter-In-Law
Carlick, Evelyne	31-Jul-51	Great Granddaughter-In-Law
Carrier, Madeleine		Granddaughter-In-Law
Chaban, Joyce Ann	2-Dec-54	Great Granddaughter-In-Law
Charlebois, Marguerite	12-Apr-42	Great Granddaughter-In-Law
Chartier, Georgina		Daughter-In-Law
Cheesman, Deanne Heather	9-May-74	2nd Great Granddaughter In Law
Chernowsky, Annette		Granddaughter-In-Law
Christie, Amber	13-Feb-07	3rd Great Granddaughter
Christie, Grace	26-Jun-03	3rd Great Grandaughter
Christie, Lance	1-Apr-76	2nd Great Grandson-In-Law
Cindy		2nd Great Granddaughter-In-Law
Clark, Brandon		3rd Great Grandson
Clark, Donna	16-Sep	2nd Great Granddaughter
Clark, Keiran		3rd Great Grandson
Clark, Stephanie		3rd Great Granddaughter
Clark, Wayne		Great Grandson-In-Law

Clark, William		2nd Great Grandson
Collins, Alyshia Leona	21-Oct-03	3rd Great Granddaughter
Collins, Lindsey Michelle	6-Jul-07	3rd Great Granddaughter
Collins, Michael	29-Aug-77	2nd Great Grandson-In-Law
Comeau, Angela Marie	21-Dec-87	3rd Great Granddaughter
Comeau, Brittany Marie	14-Dec-87	3rd Great Granddaughter
Comeau, Carly Joan	23-Mar-88	3rd Great Granddaughter
Comeau, Carrie Anne	13-Apr-83	3rd Great Granddaughter
Comeau, Christal	8-Feb-80	3rd Great Granddaughter
Comeau, Claude Eugene	26-Jan-59	2nd Great Grandson
Comeau, Claudette Marie Dianne	28-Apr-60	2nd Great Granddaughter
Comeau, Denise Raymond	17-Nov-57	2nd Great Grandson
Comeau, Gerald Paul	4-Oct-54	2nd Great Grandson
Comeau, Hector	2-Jan-31	Great Grandson-In-Law
Comeau, Jason Lee	5-Jun-75	3rd Great Grandson
Comeau, Jennifer Gail	20-Aug-74	3rd Great Granddaughter
Comeau, Kristopher Schneider	9-Sep-81	3rd Great Grandson
Comeau, Lisa Michelle	15-Jul-81	3rd Great Granddaughter
Comeau, Marcel Victor	26-May-78	3rd Great Grandson
Comeau, Michael Patrick	3-Jul-64	2nd Great Grandson
Comeau, Nicole Lynn	14-Sep-76	3rd Great Granddaughter
Comeau, Norman Hector	19-May-61	2nd Great Grandson
Comeau, Paul	25-Oct-86	3rd Great Grandson
Comeau, Rene	2-Apr-78	3rd Great Granddaughter
Comeau, Richard Louise	31-Aug-55	2nd Great Grandson
Comeau, Robyn Lyne	25-May-87	3rd Great Granddaughter
Comeau, Roger	14-Jan-63	2nd Great Grandson
Comeau, Sarah	29-Jan-92	3rd Great Granddaughter
Comeau, Sean Claude	3-Jun-89	3rd Great Grandson
Comeau, Shawna	24-Oct-83	3rd Great Granddaughter
Comeau, Shelda Anne	24-Nov-75	3rd Great Granddaughter
Comeau, Stephanie Gail	9-Feb-89	3rd Great Granddaughter
Comeau, Tina Marie Gail	6-Jun-74	3rd Great Granddaughter
Comeau, Victor Phillip	9-Aug-56	2nd Great Grandson
Coons, Karen	17-Nov-57	2nd Great Granddaughter-In-Law
Coons, Marie	8-Feb-58	2nd Great Granddaughter-In-Law

Coons, Shelda Ann	20-Jan-59	2nd Great Granddaughter-In-Law
Courturier, April Ann	25-Jan-78	2nd Great Granddaughter
Courturier, Arthur	9-Apr-28	Grandson-In-Law
Courturier, Felix Arthur Henry Joseph	18-Apr-55	Great Grandson
Courturier, Jimmy Dean	4-Mar-69	Great Grandson
Courturier, Kathleen Marie Bernadette	17-Jan-58	Great Granddaughter
Courturier, Terry Paul Victor	15-May-64	Great Grandson
Couturier, Jeanette	16-Apr-78	2nd Great Granddaughter
Couturier, Madelene	29-Sep-79	2nd Great Granddaughter
Couturier, Martina	22-Dec-74	2nd Great Granddaughter
Couturier, Richard	15-Aug-59	Great Grandson-In-Law
Dainne		2nd Great Granddaughter-In-Law
D'Andrea, John		Great Grandson-In-Law
D'Andrea, Troy		2nd Great Grandson
Davidson, Alicia	26-Sep-83	2nd Great Granddaughter
Davidson, Ashley Marie	18-Feb-87	2nd Great Granddaughter
Davidson, Brian William George	20-Oct-60	Great Grandson-In-Law
Davidson, Jamie Lynn	3-Jun-84	2nd Great Granddaughter
Davidson, Larry Grant	7-Mar-62	Great Grandson-In-Law
Davidson, Mathew James Ray	7-Jun-89	2nd Great Grandson
Davidson, Tanya Ann	28-Sep-82	2nd Great Granddaughter
Davies, David Wayne		Great Grandson-In-Law
Davies, Rose Mary		Great Granddaughter-In-Law
Dean		Great Grandson-In-Law
Delorme, Christopher	21-Sep-88	2nd Great Grandson
Delorme, Gary	11-Jun-49	Great Grandson
Delorme, Jeff	28-Aug-82	2nd Great Grandson
Delorme, John	12-Dec-52	Great Grandson
Delorme, Kelly	1-Sep-91	2nd Great Grandson
Delorme, Laurie	20-Feb-74	2nd Great Granddaughter
Delorme, Lawrence	6-Jan-26	Grandson-In-Law
Delorme, Michael	6-Nov-71	2nd Great Grandson
Denness, Austin Emerson	29-Jun-04	3rd Great Grandson

Denness, Charles Edward	19-Feb-59	Great Grandson-In-Law
Denness, Steven Fredrick	9-Jan-81	2nd Great Grandson
Deters, A.		Granddaughter-In-Law
Detillieux, Chantelle		2nd Great Granddaughter
Detillieux, Rene		Great Grandson-In-Law
Detillieux, Wendy		2nd Great Granddaughter
Dick, Cheryl	31-Mar-66	Great Granddaughter-In-Law
Doll, Clayton	3-Feb-83	2nd Great Grandson-In-Law
Dott, Callum Charles	2-Sep-96	3rd Great Grandson
Dott, Grant	28-Dec-64	2nd Great Grandson-In-Law
Ducharme, Talia Lynn-Marie	29-May-98	3rd Great Granddaughter
Ducharme, Teagan Emily Marie	15-Aug-05	3rd Great Granddaughter
Ducharme, Trevor	24-Sep-80	2nd Great Grandson-In-Law
Ducharme, Trinity Emily	31-Dec-00	3rd Great Granddaughter
Duff, Etta	10-Jun-52	Great Granddaughter-In-Law
Dumont, Adam	3-Nov-84	2nd Great Grandson
Dumont, Aiden	14-Jun-00	2nd Great Grandson
Dumont, Aurel	28-Nov-96	2nd Great Granddaughter
Dumont, Camile	14-Jun-99	2nd Great Granddaughter
Dumont, Dekota	14-Dec-98	2nd Great Grandson
Dumont, Denis Arestride	13-Feb-52	Great Grandson
Dumont, Jeannie	2-Feb-6	2 Great Granddaughter
Dumont, Jessica	28-Jan-77	2nd Great Granddaughter
Dumont, Kenneth John	22-May-58	Great Grandson
Dumont, Leo	12-Jan-30	Grandson-In-Law
Dumont, Leonard Clement	17-Aug-53	Great Grandson
Dumont, Leslie	28-Apr-77	2nd Great Granddaughter
Dumont, Lorraine Ann	28-Nov-54	Great Granddaughter
Dumont, Lorretta	14-May-80	2nd Great Granddaughter
Dumont, Marisa	8-Aug-89	2nd Great Granddaughter
Dumont, Martin John	14-Oct-64	Great Grandson
Dumont, Michele	9-Dec-74	2nd Great Granddaughter
Dumont, Rene Ernest	18-Sep-59	Great Grandson
Dumont, Roger Jules Eugene	9-Oct-50	Great Grandson
Dumont, Ryan	18-Jul-88	2nd Great Grandson

Dumont, Travis	16-Apr-86	2nd GreatGrandson
Dumont, Zac	13-Jun-82	2nd GreatGrandson
Elkhorn, Trish	9-Mar-64	Great Granddaughter-In-Law
Ethier, Alex	30-Jun-02	Son-In-Law
Ethier, Aline Marie	29-Jul-51	Great Granddaughter
Ethier, Andre	4-Nov-30	Grandson
Ethier, Anita Marie Cecile	19-Sep-37	Great Granddaughter
Ethier, Blaine Allan	3-Mar-70	2nd Great Grandson
Ethier, Brian Edward	3-Mar-70	2nd Great Grandson
Ethier, Brian		Great Grandson
Ethier, Christopher-Colin	20-Jun-72	2nd Great Grandson
Ethier, Clarence	18-Apr-41	Grandson
Ethier, Claudette Audrey Vivian	17-Feb-46	Great Granddaughter
Ethier, Coleen		Great Granddaughter
Ethier, Colette		Great Granddaughter
Ethier, Connie Lee	17-Nov-65	2nd Great Granddaughter
Ethier, Curtis Wade	17-Mar-71	2nd Great Grandson
Ethier, Daniel	11-Mar-45	Grandson
Ethier, Daryl		Great Grandson
Ethier, Denise Marie	18-May-44	Great Granddaughter
Ethier, Derek		Great Granddaughter
Ethier, Dylan Martins	9-Sep-02	3rd Great Grandson
Ethier, Edouard Charles Maurice	6-Jan-39	Great Grandson
Ethier, Eugene	23-Nov-28	Grandson
Ethier, Georgcine		Granddaughter
Ethier, Jean	15-Jan-40	Great Granddaughter
Ethier, Jeffrey Mark	18-Jan-75	2nd Great Grandson
Ethier, Kelly	2-Jan-69	Great Granddaughter
Ethier, Larry Wade	8-Jan-61	2nd Great Grandson
Ethier, Laura		Granddaughter
Ethier, Lawrence	31-May-64	Great Grandson
Ethier, Leo	29-Jul-45	Great Grandson
Ethier, Leonard Ronald	3-Oct-37	Great Grandson
Ethier, Louise	7-May-14	Grandson-In-Law
Ethier, Mary Irene	15-Sep-24	Granddaughter-In-Law
Ethier, Maurice Joseph	21-Apr-49	Great Grandson

Ethier, Norman	4-Apr-36	Grandson
Ethier, Robert Alderic	30-Jun-15	Grandson In Law
Ethier, Roger	12-Oct-65	Great Grandson
Ethier, Ronald Russell	31-Dec-40	Great Grandson
Ethier, Scott Martins	10-Feb-08	3rd Great Grandson
Ethier, Sean Colin	17-May-71	2nd Great Grandson
Ethier, William Wayne	12-Jan-58	2nd Great Grandson
Evelyn		Great Granddaughter-In-Law
Farmer, Denna	19-Feb-65	Great Granddaughter-In-Law
Ferguson, Bruce		Great Grandson-In-Law
Ferguson, Carolyne		2nd Great Granddaughter
Ferguson, Cassandra Marie	3-Feb-91	3rd Great Granddaughter
Ferguson, Christopher Scott	17-Aug-91	3rd Great Grandson
Ferguson, Darleen		2nd Great Granddaughter
Ferguson, Elaine		2nd Great Granddaughter
Ferguson, Laurie Ann		2nd Great Granddaughter
Ferguson, Scott	1969	2nd Great Grandson
Ferguson, Gary		3rd Great Grandson
Ferguson, Greg		3rd Great Grandson
Ferguson, Roy		2nd Great Grandson-In-Law
Ferguson, William		2nd Great Grandson
Ferguson, William Gorden		Great Grandson-In-Law
Ferraton, Brandon	22-Jul-86	2nd Great Grandson
Ferraton, Jeff	22-Jun-62	Great Grandson-In-Law
Foss, Gregg	6-May-56	2nd Great Grandson-In-Law
Franklin, Aybarie Samantha	19-Apr-99	3rd Great Granddaughter
Franklin, Jeffery		2nd Great Grandson-In-Law
Fugle, Billy Jean		Great Granddaughter-In-Law
Fuhr, Scott	Jun-73	3rd Great Grandson-In-Law
Gallant, Brian		2nd Great Grandson-In-Law
Gallant, Ebanie Savanah	14-Dec-94	3rd Great Granddaughter
Gartner, Terri		Great Granddaughter-In-Law
Gattacea, Daniel Vincent	11-Mar-98	4th Great Grandson
Gattacea, Gabe		3rd Great Grandson-In-Law
Gattacea, Kristen Gail	10-Mar-97	4th Great Granddaughter
Gauthier, Norma		2nd Great Granddaughter-In-Law
Gorieu, Marcel		Grandson-In-Law

Gray, Joseph Arthur		Great Grandson-In-Law
Greer, Carlene	4-Aug-70	2nd Great Granddaughter-In-Law
Greyeyes, Marie Annette	3-Feb-38	Granddaughter-In-Law
Guillet, Agnes	22-Sep-21	Granddaughter
Guillet, Alexis		Son
Guillet, Alice Gabrielle	18-May-16	Granddaughter
Guillet, Aline	26-Mar-33	Granddaughter
Guillet, Aline	19-Jun-57	Great Granddaughter
Guillet, Andre Victor	7-May-79	2nd Great Grandson
Guillet, Andrea Vandrees	12-May-82	2nd Great Granddaughter
Guillet, Angie	28-Apr-47	Great Granddaughter
Guillet, Aristide	1883	Son
Guillet, Ashley Irene Ida	15-Sep-85	2nd Great Granddaughter
Guillet, Belinda Ann	3-Jul-59	Great Granddaughter
Guillet, Boston Rain	13-Sep-05	3rd Great Grandson
Guillet, Brailee Rae	14-Jul-03	3rd Great Granddaughter
Guillet, Brandy Rae	19-Jun-81	2nd Great Granddaughter
Guillet, Bridget Jeanette	6-Sep-67	2nd Great Granddaughter
Guillet, Camille	15-Aug-00	Daughter
Guillet, Candice Gail	6-Jul-85	2nd Great Granddaughter
Guillet, Carol Marie	17-May-49	Great Granddaughter
Guillet, Catherine	4-Jun-64	Great Granddaughter
Guillet, Chantelle	9-Oct-76	2nd Great Granddaughter
Guillet, Christine	16-Nov-74	2nd Great Granddaughter
Guillet, Christopher	19-Apr-76	2nd Great Grandson
Guillet, Christopher Dennis	28-Oct-72	2nd Great Grandson
Guillet, Cindy Darlene	17-Aug-78	2nd Great Granddaughter
Guillet, Clement	1890	Son
Guillet, Clement	21-Feb-22	Grandson
Guillet, Collin Bradly	11-May-95	2nd Great Grandson
Guillet, Collin Rene	27-Feb-80	2nd Great Grandson
Guillet, Corey James	22-May-87	2nd Great Grandson
Guillet, Daniel	13-Mar-50	Great Grandson
Guillet, Danielle Lynn	20-Aug-82	2nd Great Granddaughter
Guillet, Darlene		Great Granddaughter
Guillet, Darlene	26-Nov-49	Great Granddaughter
Guillet, Dawn Lee	14-Oct-71	2nd Great Granddaughter

Guillet, Debra Jeanette	5-Dec-56	Great Granddaughter
Guillet, Denis		Great Grandson
Guillet, Denise		Great Grandson
Guillet, Denise	1925	Granddaughter
Guillet, Denise	19-Apr-69	Great Granddaughter
Guillet, Dennis		Great Granddaughter
Guillet, Dennis Edward Norman	18-Jan-44	Great Grandson
Guillet, Diane		Great Granddaughter
Guillet, Donald Lorne	3-Dec-46	Great Grandson
Guillet, Dorina	3-Sep-46	Great Granddaughter
Guillet, Edmond	27-Nov-19	Grandson
Guillet, Edward	20-Oct-19	Grandson
Guillet, Edward Maurice Jr.	10-Oct-61	Great Grandson
Guillet, Elaina Aline Darlene	26-Sep-64	Great Granddaughter
Guillet, Elise Marie Rollande	21-Sep-23	Granddaughter
Guillet, Ella Violet Joy	2-Jan-04	2nd Great Granddaughter
Guillet, Ernest Henry	20-Sep-45	Great Grandson
Guillet, Ernest William Edward	3-Oct-65	2nd Great Grandson
Guillet, Eugene Leon	23 May 1894	Son
Guillet, Eugene Raymond	1-Oct-56	Great Grandson
Guillet, Evan Kenneth Edward	10-Aug-06	2nd Great Grandson
Guillet, Evelyne		Great Granddaughter
Guillet, Faye Maureena	13-Apr-70	Great Granddaughter
Guillet, Felix	14-Jul-27	Grandson
Guillet, Florence	1928	Granddaughter
Guillet, Frances	8-Jan-26	Granddaughter
Guillet, Francois	2 Jan 1854	Self
Guillet, Francois	1880	Son
Guillet, Gabrielle	1-Apr-18	Granddaughter
Guillet, George	29-Jun	Great Grandson
Guillet, Gerald	27-Jul-49	Great Grandson
Guillet, Gilbert	13-Nov-22	Grandson
Guillet, Helen	1914	Granddaughter

Guillet, Henri Francois	11 Sep 1889	Son
Guillet, Henriette	4-Jun-15	Granddaughter
Guillet, Irene	12-May-28	Granddaughter
Guillet, Irene	26-Oct-50	Great Granddaughter
Guillet, Janice Laurelle	3-Jun-60	Great Granddaughter
Guillet, Jeannie Lynn	22-Mar-82	2nd Great Granddaughter
Guillet, Jocelyn		Great Granddaughter
Guillet, Johnny	8-Aug-24	Grandson
Guillet, Kevin Joseph	10-Apr-65	Great Grandson
Guillet, Kieriana Alyssa	30-Dec-07	3rd Great Granddaughter
Guillet, Kyle Luc	1-Apr-93	2nd Great Grandson
Guillet, Lauence		Great Grandson
Guillet, Laurana Nicole	22-Nov-05	3rd Great Granddaughter
Guillet, Lawrence	21-Jan-54	Great Grandson
Guillet, Lawrence Larry		Great Grandson
Guillet, Leon	8-May-30	Grandson
Guillet, Leona Frances	5-Jul-58	Great Granddaughter
Guillet, Leslie Gordon	8-Oct-47	Great Grandson
Guillet, Linda	27-Jun-58	Great Granddaughter
Guillet, Lisa Marie	6-Feb-68	2nd Great Granddaughter
Guillet, Lisa Marie	25-Jul-81	2nd Great Granddaughter
Guillet, Lorraine	29-Dec 35	Granddaughter
Guillet, Louis	12 Mar 1898	Daughter
Guillet, Lucille M.	10-Feb-51	Great Granddaughter
Guillet, Marcel		Great Granddaughter
Guillet, Marcel	31-Oct-22	Grandson
Guillet, Mark Harold	18-Nov-63	Great Grandson
Guillet, Marthe	7 Sep 1884	Daughter
Guillet, Maurice	1-Jan-57	Great Grandson-In-Law
Guillet, Maurice	24-Jun-59	Great Grandson
Guillet, Maxime Edward Leslie	25-Aug-74	2nd Great Grandson
Guillet, Michael Gordon Jerald	25-Sep-77	2nd Great Grandson
Guillet, Michelle Clement	2-Aug-90	2nd Great Grandson
Guillet, Michelle Marie	9-Jan-86	2nd Great Granddaughter
Guillet, Norman		Great Grandson
Guillet, Norman Daryl	4-Jul-55	Great Grandson

Guillet, Paul Ernest	22-May-51	Grandson
Guillet, Ramona Marie	6-Jan-61	Great Granddaughter
Guillet, Raymond		Great Grandson
Guillet, Raymond Albert	6-Sep-36	Grandson
Guillet, Raymond Cecil		Great Grandson
Guillet, Richard	25-Jul-56	Great Grandson
Guillet, Rita	13-May-53	Great Granddaughter
Guillet, Robert	20-Mar-39	Great Grandson
Guillet, Robert	17-May-52	Great Grandson
Guillet, Ronald Francis	5-May-52	Great Grandson
Guillet, Ryan Cyril	10-Dec-83	2nd Great Grandson
Guillet, Sandra Lynn	31-Jul-58	Great Granddaughter
Guillet, Scott	16-Mar-78	2nd Great Grandson
Guillet, Sharon	7-Feb-66	Great Granddaughter
Guillet, Sharyn Edith Dianne	14-Jun-49	Great Granddaughter
Guillet, Shelbie Audrianna	14-Mar-90	2nd Great Granddaughter
Guillet, Suzanne		Great Granddaughter
Guillet, Tammy Lynne	28-Mar-69	2nd Great Granddaughter
Guillet, Tanner Gary	23-Aug-91	2nd Great Grandson
Guillet, Theresa Simone	26-Nov-71	2nd Great Granddaughter
Guillet, Travis Edward David	5-Mar-88	2nd Great Grandson
Guillet, Tyler James	30-Apr-86	2nd Great Grandson
Guillet, Victor	12-Apr-62	Great Grandson
Guillet, Walter	1912	Grandson
Guillet, Yvonne		Granddaughter
Hagerman, Becky-Jo	22-Jun-80	2nd Great Granddaughter-In-Law
Haggard, Rodney	23-Aug-70	Great Grandson-In-Law
Hale, Jennifer Mae		2nd Great Granddaughter-In-Law
Hall, Jeff	26-Sep-66	Great Grandson-In-Law
Hall, Jesse	19-Jan-91	2nd Great Grandson
Hall, Lucus	14-Feb-94	2nd Great Grandson
Hamel, Emilienne Bell	2-Mar-99	2nd Great Granddaughter
Hamel, Evelyn	3-Jun-50	Great Granddaughter
Hamel, Jacqueline Jean	7-Jan-54	Great Granddaughter
Hamel, Kiera Julianne	9-Nov-01	2nd Great Granddaughter
Hamel, Leo Paul Marcel	22-Dec-17	Grandson-In-Law

Hamel, Ronald Robert	12-Jan-61	Great Grandson
Hanusz, Nancy	24-Oct-46	Great Granddaughter-In-Law
Hauk, Debra Joan		Great Granddaughter In Law
Haw, Connie-Jo	13-Jul-77	2nd Great Granddaughter
Haw, Gordon Wayne	14-Mar-47	Great Grandson-In-Law
Haw, Nicole	2-May-70	2nd Great Granddaughter
Haw, Wayne Albert	14-Feb-74	2nd Great Grandson
Hegedus, Bryan	3-Mar-77	2nd Great Grandson
Hegedus, Edwin Lyle		Foster Great Grandson-In-Law
Hegedus, Ryan	27-May-79	2nd Great Grandson
Heroux, Cory John	7-Sep-94	2nd Great Grandson
Hnidy, Carol		Great Granddaughter-In-Law
Hoffensetz, Arne		Great Grandson-In-Law
Houle, Yvette		Granddaughter-In-Law
Hrapchak, Kimberly		2nd Great Granddaughter
Hrapchak, Les		2nd Great Grandson
Hrapchak, Stephan		Great Grandson-In-Law
Hrapchak, Wes		2nd Great Grandson
Hudson, Linda Mary	8-Aug-50	Great Granddaughter-In-Law
Hynes, Rylee Lee	15-Jun-88	3rd Great Grandson
Hynes, Shawn		2nd Great Grandson-In-Law
Ireland, David Anthony	11-Mar-86	2nd Great Grandson
Ireland, Nicholas Alexander	27-Feb-83	2nd Great Grandson
Irving, Cerise		2nd Great Grandson-In-Law
Iverson, Iris Dianne		Great Granddaughter-In-Law
James, Melanie Gladys Joy	30-Sep-70	Great Granddaughter-In-Law
Janner, Mary	11-Dec-29	Granddaughter-In-Law
Jolin, Coltin	17-Dec-92	3rd Great Grandson
Jolin, Daniel Will Jr.		2nd Great Grandson In Law
Jolin, Quinton	14-Aug-94	3rd Great Grandson
Joubert, Jeanne Marie	21 Jun 1896	Daughter-In-Law
Joubert, Rolande	24-Aug-01	Son-In-Law
Juliette		Granddaughter-In-Law
Keizer, Natalie	9-Jun-77	2nd Great Granddaughter-In-Law
Kennedy, Gail	22-Apr-55	Great Granddaughter-In-Law
Klassen, Joryn	8-Aug-97	3rd Great Grandson
Klassen, Kelly Nathan	13-Jun-75	2nd Great Grandson-In-Law

Klassen, Rayelle	4-Feb-00	3rd Great Granddaughter
Kolody, Brice	16-Jun-01	4th Great Grandson
Kolody, Hanna	14-Dec-02	4th Great Granddaughter
Kolody, Joshua	27-Oct-99	4th Great Grandson
Kolody, Kristen	7-Dec-97	4th Great Granddaughter
Kolody, Randy		3rd Great Grandson-In-Law
Kolosky, Jamie Donald	6-Apr-88	3rd Great Grandson
Kolosky, Jeris John	14-Sep-86	3rd Great Grandson
Kolosky, John William	10-Nov-60	2nd Great Grandson-In-Law
Kuhtey, April	21-Apr-75	2nd Great Granddaughter-In-Law
Kustaski, Colleen		Great Granddaughter
Kustaski, Elaine		Great Granddaughter
Kustaski, Garry		Great Grandson
Kustaski, George		Grandson-In-Law
Kustaski, Jordan		2nd Great Grandson
Kustaski, Laurisa		2nd Great Granddaughter
Kustaski, Linda		Great Granddaughter
Kustaski, Lori Ann		Great Granddaughter
Kustaski, Robert		Great Grandson
Kustaski, Vern		Great Grandson
Kyle, Deborah Ann		Great Granddaughter-In-Law
Laird, Judy	22-Oct-52	Great Granddaughter-In-Law
Larson, Karen		Great Granddaughter-In-Law
Legault		Grandson-In-Law
Legault, Robert		Great Grandson
LeHaye, Dianna		Great Granddaughter-In-Law
Lepage, Wilfred	28-Jan-20	Grandson-In-Law
Lepine, Therese	29-Apr	Granddaughter-In-Law
Lequalt, Maria	12 Apr 1896	Daughter-In-Law
Lesliel Guillet, Steven	16-Jul-01	3rd Great Grandson
Lestage, Albert Joseph	8-May-28	Grandson-In-Law
Lestage, Arron Michal	11-Jun-91	3rd Great Grandson
Lestage, Art	2-Nov-31	Great Grandson-In-Law
Lestage, Claudette Lorette	1-Jun-58	Great Granddaughter
Lestage, Cole		3rd Great Grandson
Lestage, Dale	20-Jun-62	2nd Great Grandson
Lestage, Damond James	23-Apr-91	2nd Great Grandson

Lestage, Darcy	6-Aug-80	2nd Great Grandson
Lestage, Darrell	3-Oct-63	2nd Great Grandson
Lestage, David	3-Oct-63	2nd Great Grandson
Lestage, Deanna	15-Aug-60	2nd Great Granddaughter
Lestage, Dwayne	1-Jan-66	2nd Great Grandson
Lestage, Gary Glenn	28-Nov-54	Great Grandson
Lestage, Gregory Leslie	4-Jul-59	Great Grandson
Lestage, Kayleigh	13-Nov-88	2nd Great Granddaughter
Lestage, Nola	30-Jul-76	2nd Great Granddaughter
Lestage, Rodney Drew	9-May-65	Great Grandson
Lestage, Roland Albert	22-Dec-53	Great Grandson
Lestage, Ryan	20-Jul-77	2nd Great Grandson
Lestage, Valerie Angie	10-Jul-74	Great Granddaughter
Licthenwald, Judy	11-Sep-52	Great Granddaughter-In-Law
Littlejohn, Crystal	12-Jun-83	2nd Great Granddaughter-In-Law
Lizotte, Curtis Rubin		2nd Great Grandson-In-Law
Lizotte, Erin Simone	14-Apr-96	3rd Great Granddaughter
Lizotte, Jenna Marie	31-Oct-97	3rd Great Granddaughter
Lizotte, Kristen Emily	17-Feb-95	3rd Great Granddaughter
Maiser, Pat		Great Granddaughter-In-Law
Maisey, Keith William	21-Feb-72	2nd Great Grandson-In-Law
Maisey, Loula Sophia	9-Oct-07	3rd Great Granddaughter
Mareschal, Renee	11-May-72	2nd Great Grandson
Mareschal, Terry	2-Jun-45	Great Grandson-In-Law
Mareschal, Warren	18-Nov-74	2nd Great Grandson
Martins, Antonieta	5-Apr-72	2nd Great Granddaughter-In-Law
Mason, Krista Marie	5-Dec-01	3rd Great Granddaughter
Mason, Richard	7-Dec-75	2nd Great Grandson-In-Law
Matheson, Aaron		3rd Great Grandson-In-Law
Matheson, Brandon Lee	13-Jan-93	4th Great Grandson
Matheson, Braydon	24-Aug-96	4th Great Grandson
Matheson, Jordan	18-Jun-99	4th Great Grandson
McFatridge, Dylan	10-Jul-02	4th Great Grandson
McFatridge, Ian	10-May-76	3rd Great Grandson-In-Law
McFatridge, Jayce	30-Nov-04	4th Great Grandson
McLaren, Kevin		2nd Great Grandson-In-Law
McLaren, Reese William	7-Oct-06	3rd Great Grandson

McQuigge, Penny		Great Granddaughter-In-Law
Mercredi, Jane	12-May-55	Great Granddaughter-In-Law
Miller, Anthony	14-Sep-98	3rd Great Grandson
Miller, Dilon	5-Jun-95	3rd Great Grandson
Miller, John	30-Nov-72	2nd Great Grandson-In-Law
Moore, Vicky Helen	23-Nov-64	Great Granddaughter-In-Law
Moxam, Marjorie Rae	2-Feb-40	Great Granddaughter-In-Law
Nelson, Eric	22-Aug-53	Great Grandson-In-Law
Nelson, John Bowman	9-Nov-44	Great Grandson-In-Law
Nelson, Michel Victor	25-Oct-77	2nd Great Granddaughter
Nelson, Michelle Marie	1-Jan-72	2nd Great Granddaughter
Nesdoly, Theresa	5-Apr-65	2nd Great Granddaughter-In-Law
Nodge, James	9-Dec-53	Great Grandson-In-Law
Nodge, Jocelyn Jean	17-Aug-83	2nd Great Granddaughter
Nodge, Robert Paul	23-Dec-87	2nd Great Grandson
Nodge, Theodore James	8-Apr-85	2nd Great Grandson
Pacholik, Barbara Ann	23-Oct-65	Great Granddaughter-In-Law
Papp, Daryl		Great Grandson-In-Law
Parker, Loreen	25-Apr-58	Great Granddaughter-In-Law
Paul, Dianne	10-Aug-48	Great Granddaughter-In-Law
Petz, Angeline	2-Feb-76	2nd Great Granddaughter
Petz, Derek	13-Dec-79	2nd Great Grandson
Petz, Douglas		Great Grandson-In-Law
Petz, Kaleb	31-Mar-02	3rd Great Grandson
Phaneuf, Emile		Great Grandson-In-Law
Phaneuf, Meka Joseph	5-Sep-74	2nd Great Grandson
Phaneuf, Mia	1972	2nd Great Granddaughter
Pilon, Angeline Georgine	8-Dec-00	Daughter-In-Law
Plamondon, Barbara		2nd Great Granddaughter-In-Law
Pluchon		Father-In-Law
Pluchon, Marie	31 Mar 1857	Wife
Podolecki, Jenna	8-Jun-93	3rd Great Granddaughter
Podolecki, Michael Peter	1-Apr-63	2nd Great Grandson
Podolecki, Patricia Anne	3-May-62	2nd Great Granddaughter
Podolecki, Peter	2-Jun-39	Great Grandson-In-Law
Podolecki, Richard Matthew	6-Jun-64	2nd Great Grandson
Podolecki, Stephen	25-May-91	3rd Great Grandson

Podolecki, Teresa	27-Jul-65	2nd Great Granddaughter
Poitras, Marquerite	1-Apr-26	Granddaughter-In-Law
Pounder, Allan		Great Grandson-In-Law
Prefontaine, Daniel	5-Aug-40	Great Grandson
Prefontaine, Lisa	15-Dec-65	2nd Great Granddaughter
Prefontaine, Nicole	22-Nov-64	2nd Great Granddaughter
Prefontaine, Rachelle	26-Feb-68	2nd Great Granddaughter
Prefontaine, Sylvia Bertha Marie	9-Nov-44	Great Granddaughter
Prefontaine, Victor	8-Apr-17	Grandson-In-Law
Purschke, Sharon Ann	16-Oct-58	Great Grand daughter-In-Law
Pylypchuk, Dean Curtis	23-Jan-82	2nd Great Grandson
Pylypchuk, Leanne Michelle	1-Feb-86	2nd Great Granddaughter
Pylypchuk, Michael	23-Jul-52	Great Grandson-In-Law
Rabut, Hubert Remi		Great Grandson-In-Law
Reed, Shelley	5-Aug-57	Great Granddaughter-In-Law
Reslein, Kristin	23-Feb-79	2nd Great Granddaughter-In-Law
Robert, Darcy	15-Aug-85	2nd Great Grandson
Robert, Leanne	16-Nov-81	2nd Great Granddaughter
Robert, Paul	4-Oct-63	2nd Great Grandson-In-Law
Robert, Tammy	7-May-79	2nd Great Granddaughter
Robertson, Sandra Joan		Great Granddaughter-In-Law
Ross		Great Grandson-In-Law
Ross, Kerry Louise	Jan-78	2nd Great Granddaughter
Roy, Henri		Grandson-In-Law
Roy, Marie Louise		Granddaughter-In-Law
Sarrasin, Augustine	5-Mar-41	Great Granddaughter
Sarrasin, Dorothy		2nd Great Granddaughter
Sarrasin, Elaine Frances		Great Granddaughter
Sarrasin, Eugene		Great Grandson
Sarrasin, Evelyn Margaret		Great Granddaughter
Sarrasin, Girl		2nd Great Granddaughter
Sarrasin, Girl1		2nd Great Granddaughter
Sarrasin, Jackie		2nd Great Granddaughter
Sarrasin, Jeannette		Great Granddaughter
Sarrasin, Jo-Lan		2nd Great Granddaughter
Sarrasin, Joseph Albert		Grandson-In-Law

Sarrasin, Kevin		2nd Great Grandson
Sarrasin, Lawrence		Great Grandson
Sarrasin, Louise		Great Granddaughter
Sarrasin, Margaret		Great Granddaughter
Sarrasin, Marie		Great Granddaughter
Sarrasin, Vivian		Great Granddaughter
Schafeor, Kay	15-Feb-28	Granddaughter-In-Law
Schilling, Rhonda	22-Sep-75	2nd Great Granddaughter-In-Law
Schlosser, Harley		Great Grandson-In-Law
Schneider, Maureen	19-Apr-64	2nd Great Granddaughter-In-Law
Schonwald, Braidon Kenden	14-Dec-95	3rd Great Grandson
Schonwald, James Melvin		2nd Great Grandson-In-Law
Schonwald, Megan Mary-Lynn	21-Jan-91	3rd Great Granddaughter
Schonwald, Rialey-Ann Paige	31-Aug-92	3rd Great Granddaughter
Seegerts, Teena	8-Jan-57	Foster GreatGranddaughter
Seidel, Sharlene Jeanette	25-Jun-51	Great Granddaughter-In-Law
Shaw, Lana		Great Granddaughter-In-Law
Sheila		2nd Great Granddaughter-In-Law
Shevkenek, Kennedy Adele	21-Jun-04	3rd Great Grandson
Shevkenek, Loni James	22-Mar-77	2nd Great Grandson
Shevkenek, Robert James	1-Dec-56	Great Grandson-In-Law
Shevkenek, Sheldon Grayson James	9-Aug-06	3rd Great Grandson
Shevkenek, Trudy Lynn	30-Aug-78	2nd Great Granddaughter
Smith, Colbie James	31-Oct-86	3rd Great Grandson
Smith, Jim		2nd Great Grandson-In-Law
Solonenko, Sonia		Granddaughter-In-Law
Spiers, Cale Lorne	12-Jul-83	2nd Great Grandson
Spiers, Devon Nancy	24-Aug-89	2nd Great Grandson
Spiers, Mervine Lorne		Great Grandson-In-Law
Stamnschroer, Erica Ann	22-Aug-53	Great Granddaughter-In-Law
Steen, Fredrick Ivan	27-Jul-68	2nd Great Grandson-In-Law
Steen, Presley Sharlene	8-Sep-00	3rd Great Granddaughter
Stone		Grandson-In-Law
Szabo, Andrea Marie	24-Sep-59	Great Granddaughter-In-Law
Szelecz, Arnold		2nd Great Grandson-In-Law

Szelecz, Dennis Joseph	22-Jul-99	3rd Great Grandson
Tammy		2nd Great Granddaughter-In-Law
Tedlock, Levi	7-Dec-01	2nd Great Grandson
Tedlock, Wayne		Great Grandson-In-Law
Tessier, Orphir		Grandson-In-Law
Theoret, Jeanne		Great Granddaughter-In-Law
Tobin, Joyce	11-Apr-51	Great Granddaughter-In-Law
Treland, Roger Allan	1-Mar-53	Great Grandson-In-Law
Vedress, Janet	20-Dec	Great Granddaughter-In-Law
Villeneuve		Grandson-In-Law
Villeneuve, Paulette		Great Granddaughter
Viola, Jenny		2nd Great Granddaughter
Viola, Vince Andrea		Great Grandson-In-Law
Wallace, Elaine	16-Jun-68	2nd Great Granddaughter-In-Law
Watson, Brent	6-Feb-82	2nd Great Grandson
Watson, Charles Allan	8-Dec-62	Great Grandson-In-Law
Watson, Colin Chuck	22-Oct-52	Great Grandson-In-Law
Watson, Colleen	1-Jun-80	2nd Great Granddaughter
Weber, Daniel Lawrence	27-Jul-90	2nd Great Grandson
Weber, Jim		Great Grandson-In-Law
Wester, Elizabeth	29-Sep-53	Great Granddaughter-In-Law
Whiting, Cassandra	18-Dec-79	3rd Great Granddaughter-In-Law
Wielgosz, Eric	20-Jun-81	3rd Great Grandson
Wielgosz, Landen Cole	30-Aug-03	4th Great Grandson
Wielgosz, Larry	13-Apr-57	2nd Great Grandson-In-Law
Wielgosz, Mark	25-Oct-79	3rd Great Grandson
Wielgosz, Taylin	4-Jun-01	4th Great Granddaughter
Wilde, Patrick Paul		3rd Great Grandson-In-Law
Williams, Louise		Granddaughter-In-Law
Wilson, Donna		Great Granddaughter-In-Law
Wittstruck, Colin James	20-Aug-73	2nd Great Grandson
Wittstruck, Edward	4-Oct-51	Great Grandson-In-Law
Wittstruck, Jason Edward	14-Jun-76	2nd Great Grandson
Wittstruck, Kenneth James	1-Jul-69	2nd Great Grandson
Wittstruck, Vanessa Laurea	13-Dec-97	3rd Great Granddaughter
Wolff, Mark		2nd Great Granddaughter-In-Law
Wood, Connie Francis	6-Jan-58	Great Granddaughter-In-Law

Xavier, Leon		2nd Great Grandson-In-Law
Young, Alexander Sage	3-Jan-91	2nd Great Grandson
Young, Dave		Great Grandson-In-Law
Yuzik, Josephine	10-Mar-31	Granddaughter-In-Law
Zayha-Aseltine, Betty	17-Oct-37	Great Granddaughter-In-Law

SOURCE:

Ancestry.com, 1901 Census of Canada (Provo, UT, USA: The Generations Network, Inc., 2006), www.ancestry.com, Online publication-Ancestry.com. 1901 Census of Canada [database on-line]. Provo, UT, USA: The Generations Network, Inc., 2006.Original data-Library and Archives Canada. Census of Canada, 1901. Ottawa, Canada: Library and Archives Canada, RG31, T-6428 to T-6556.

Harvest of memories 1889-1995
Domremy History Book

Information writen on old pictures

Family submissions

The Jean Carrier Family

Decendants of Jean Carrier

GENERATION 1

1. Jean Carrier-1. He married Jeanne Dodier.

   Child of Jean Carrier and Jeanne Dodier is:
   2.   i.   Charles Carrier.

GENERATION 2

2. Child of Charles Carrier and Barbe Hally is:
   3.   i.   Charles Carrier.

GENERATION 3

3. Charles Carrier-3(Charles Carrier-2, Jean Carrier-1). He married Marie Gesseron.

   Child of Charles Carrier and Marie Gesseron is:
   4.   i.   Charles Carrier.

GENERATION 4

4. Charles Carrier-4(Charles Carrier-3, Charles Carrier-2, Jean Carrier-1). He married Veronique Guay.

   Child of Charles Carrier and Veronique Guay is:
   5.   i.   Charles Joseph Carrier.

GENERATION 5

5.   Charles Joseph Carrier-5(Charles Carrier-4, Charles Carrier-3, Charles Carrier-2, Jean Carrier-1). He married Marie Anne Pichet.

Child of Charles Joseph Carrier and Marie Anne Pichet is:
6.   i.   Joseph Carrier.

GENERATION 6

6.   Joseph Carrier-6(Charles Joseph Carrier-5, Charles Carrier-4, Charles Carrier-3, Charles Carrier-2, Jean Carrier-1). He married Margurite Tomereau, daughter of Nicolas Louise Tomereau and Angelique Chretien.

Child of Joseph Carrier and Margurite Tomereau is:
7.   i.   Andre Carriere.

GENERATION 7

7.   Andre Carriere-7(Joseph Carrier-6, Charles Joseph Carrier-5, Charles Carrier-4, Charles Carrier-3, Charles Carrier-2, Jean Carrier-1). He married Angelique Lyons, daughter of Thomas Dion and Woman of the Cree Nation.

Child of Andre Carriere and Angelique Lyons is:
8.   i.   Louise Carrier, B: 1813, D: 24 Jun 1875, M: 1842.

GENERATION 8

8.   Louise Carrier-8(Andre Carriere-7, Joseph Carrier-6, Charles Joseph Carrier-5, Charles Carrier-4, Charles Carrier-3, Charles Carrier-2, Jean Carrier-1) was born on 1813. She died on 24 Jun 1875. She married

Jean Baptiste Normand in 1842, son of Michel Normand and Francoise Belanger. He was born in 1810 in Red River.

Children of Louise Carrier and Jean Baptiste Normand are:
9.   i.   Angelique Lemay, B: 1798 in Rupertsland, D: Batoche, M: St. Norbert, MB.
      ii.   Moise Normand, B: Nov 1841.
10.   iii. Helen Normand, B: 1842.
      iv.   Mathias Normand, B: 1847.
      v.   Boniface Normand.
      vi.   Joseph Normand, B: 1851.
      vii. Napoleon Normand, B: 1852.

GENERATION 9

9. Angelique Lemay-9(Louise Carrier-8, Andre Carriere-7, Joseph Carrier-6, Charles Joseph Carrier-5, Charles Carrier-4, Charles Carrier-3, Charles Carrier-2, Jean Carrier-1) was born in 1798 in Rupertsland. She died in Batoche. She married Antoine Pilon in St. Norbert, MB. He was born in 1789 in St. Norbert, MB. He died in Batoche.

Children of Angelique Lemay and Antoine Pilon are:
11.   i.   Joseph Pilon, B: Aug 1837 in St. Norbert, MB, D: 25 Mar 1915 in Batoche, M: 12 Jan 1858 in St. Norbert, MB.
      ii.   Jean-Baptiste Pilon, B: 09 Dec 1832.
12.   iii. Marie Pilon, B: Jan 1840 in St. Norbert, MB, D: 29 Nov 1932 in St. Norbert, MB, M: 12 Jan 1858 in St. Norbert, MB.
      iv.   Genevieve Pilon, B: 1840.
13.   v.   Angelique Pilon, B: 1845 in St. Norbert, MB.
14.   vi.   Scholastique Pilon.
      vii. Annie Pilon, B: 1845.
      viii. Casimire Pilon, B: 1846 in St. Norbert,MB.
15.   ix.   Andre Pilon, B: 1848, M: 03 Sep 1872 in St. Norbert, MB.
      x.   William Pilon, B: 1848.

10. Helen Normand-9(Louise Carrier-8, Andre Carriere-7, Joseph Carrier-6, Charles Joseph Carrier-5, Charles Carrier-4, Charles Carrier-3, Charles Carrier-2, Jean Carrier-1) was born in 1842. She married Pierre Parenteau.

Child of Helen Normand and Pierre Parenteau is:
    i.   Marie Virgone Parenteau, B: 03 Oct 1870.

GENERATION 10

11. Joseph Pilon-10(Angelique Lemay-9, Louise Carrier-8, Andre Carriere-7, Joseph Carrier-6, Charles Joseph Carrier-5, Charles Carrier-4, Charles Carrier-3, Charles Carrier-2, Jean Carrier-1) was born in Aug 1837 in St. Norbert, MB. He died on 25 Mar 1915 in Batoche. He married Angelique Normand on 12 Jan 1858 in St. Norbert, MB, daughter of Jean-Baptiste Normand and Louise Carriere. She was born in 1839. She died in 1927.

Children of Joseph Pilon and Angelique Normand are:
       i.   Modeste Pilon.
16.   ii.   Patrice Pilon, B: 1878.
17.   iii. Joseph Pilon, B: 17 Apr 1855, D: 1941, M: 1893 in Batoche.
18.   iv. Barthelemi Pilon, B: 30 Sep 1861 in St. Norbert, Manitoba, D: 1940, M: 17 Jan 1882 in St. Boniface, MB.
      v.   Marie Pilon, B: 1867, M: 1893 in Batoche.
     vi. Albert Pilon, B: 1875.
19.   vii. Octavie Pilon, B: 1875, D: 1979, M: 1895.

12. Marie Pilon-10(Angelique Lemay-9, Louise Carrier-8, Andre Carriere-7, Joseph Carrier-6, Charles Joseph Carrier-5, Charles Carrier-4, Charles Carrier-3, Charles Carrier-2, Jean Carrier-1) was born in Jan 1840 in St. Norbert, MB. She died on 29 Nov 1932 in St. Norbert, MB. She married Alexis Lamirande on 12 Jan 1858 in St. Norbert, MB. He was born on 5 Dec 1839 in St. Norbert, MB.

Children of Marie Pilon and Alexis Lamirande are:

121

20. i. Marie Lamirande, B: 1858.
    ii. Pierre Alexander Lamirande.
21. iii. Helene Claire Clarisse Lamirande, B: 23 Dec 1870 in St. Norbert, MB, D: 12 Jan 1947, M: 28 Nov 1893 in St. Norbert, MB.
22. iv. Joseph Emery Lamirande, B: 26 Apr 1880 in St. Norbert, MB.
23. v. Margurite Lamirande, B: 05 May 1882, M: 11 Apr 1899 in St. Norbert, MB.
24. vi. Joseph-Herve Lamirande.
25. vii. Louis Lamirande.

13. Angelique Pilon-10(Angelique Lemay-9, Louise Carrier-8, Andre Carriere-7, Joseph Carrier-6, Charles Joseph Carrier-5, Charles Carrier-4, Charles Carrier-3, Charles Carrier-2, Jean Carrier-1) was born in 1845 in St. Norbert, MB. She married Joseph Normand. He was born on 01 Mar 1845 in St. Norbert, MB.

Children of Angelique Pilon and Joseph Normand are:
    i. Marie Octavie Normand, B: 09 Nov 1871 in St. Norbert, MB.
    ii. Frederic Normand, B: 13 May 1877 in St. Norbert, MB.
    iii. Alexis Normand, B: 1878.
    iv. Pierre Normand.
    v. Joseph Normand.
    vi. Angelique Normand.
    vii. Patrice Normand, B: 19 Dec 1878.
    viii. Louis Normand, B: 1883.
    ix. William Normand, B: 1885.

14. Scholastique Pilon-10(Angelique Lemay-9, Louise Carrier-8, Andre Carriere-7, Joseph Carrier-6, Charles Joseph Carrier-5, Charles Carrier-4, Charles Carrier-3, Charles Carrier-2, Jean Carrier-1). She married Thomas Frobisher. He was born in 1814 in Red River.

Children of Scholastique Pilon and Thomas Frobisher are:
    i. Rosalie Frobisher, B: 1846.

ii. Thomas Frobisher, B: 1848.

iii. Francois Frobisher, B: 1850.

iv. Elise Frobisher, B: 1852.

v. Marqurite Frobisher, B: 1854.

vi. Melanie Frobisher, B: 1856.

vii. Nancy Frobisher, B: 1858.

viii. Henry Frobisher, B: 1860.

ix. Julien Frobisher, B: 1863.

x. Alexandre Frobisher, B: 1864.

15. Andre Pilon-10(Angelique Lemay-9, Louise Carrier-8, Andre Carriere-7, Joseph Carrier-6, Charles Joseph Carrier-5, Charles Carrier-4, Charles Carrier-3, Charles Carrier-2, Jean Carrier-1) was born in 1848. He married Celina Roy on 03 Sep 1872 in St. Norbert, MB. She was born in 1853. He married Marqurite St-Germain on 27 Jul 1880 in St. Norbert, MB. She was born in Nov 1853.

Child of Andre Pilon and Celina Roy is:
    i. Marie Pilon, B: 1873.

Children of Andre Pilon and Marqurite St-Germain are:
    i. Anne Pilon, B: 1879.
    ii. Virginie Pilon.
    iii. Josephine Pilon, B: 29 Dec 1882 in St. Norbert, MB.

GENERATION 11

16. Patrice Pilon-11(Joseph Pilon-10, Angelique Lemay-9, Louise Carrier-8, Andre Carriere-7, Joseph Carrier-6, Charles Joseph Carrier-5, Charles Carrier-4, Charles Carrier-3, Charles Carrier-2, Jean Carrier-1).

    i. Alexander Pilon, B: 1864.
    ii. William Pilon, B: 1873.

17. Joseph Pilon-11(Joseph Pilon-10, Angelique Lemay-9, Louise Carrier-8, Andre Carriere-7, Joseph Carrier-6, Charles Joseph Carrier-5, Charles Carrier-4, Charles Carrier-3, Charles Carrier-2, Jean Carrier-1) was born on 17 Apr 1859. He died in 1941. He married Julienne Braconnier in 1893 in Batoche, daughter of Daniel Branconnier and Sarah Ducharme. She was born on 24 Mar 1872 in St. Agathe. She died in 1960 in Batoche, SK.

Children of Joseph Pilon and Julienne Braconnier are:

Angeline Georgine Pilon

26. i. Joe Pilon, B: 05 Jan 1893 in Gabriel's Crossing, SK, D: 10 Feb 1993, M: 1914.

27. ii. William John Pilon, B: 1898, D: 1951 a tractor rolled and pinned him.

28. iii. Angeline Georgine Pilon, B: 08 Dec 1900 in Batoche SK, D: 23 Sep 1997 in Regina SK, M: 23 Sep 1920 in Batoche SK.

29. iv. Mary Pilon, B: 24 Jun 1910 in Batoche, SK, D: 23 Feb 1981 in Saskatoon, SK.

30. v. Angelique Pilon, B: 1903, D: 1936 died at 33yrs of TB.

31. vi. Blanche Pilon.

Angelique Pilon

Juliana Pilon

Joe Pilon

18. Barthelemi Pilon-11(Joseph Pilon-10, Angelique Lemay-9, Louise Carrier-8, Andre Carriere-7, Joseph Carrier-6, Charles Joseph Carrier-5, Charles Carrier-4, Charles Carrier-3, Charles Carrier-2, Jean Carrier-1) was born on 30 Sep 1861 in St. Norbert, MB. He died in 1940. He married Christine Dumas on 17 Jan 1882 in St. Boniface, MB. She was born on 03 Jan 1862 in St. Vital, MB. She died in 1954.

Children of Barthelemi Pilon and Christine Dumas are:
  i.   Louis Alfred Pilon, B: 15 Sep 1883 in Batoche, SK.
  ii. Henri Pilon, B: 28 Apr 1888, M: 12 May 1908 in Batoche, SK.
  iii. George Pilon, B: 05 Dec 1900 in Batoche, SK, M: 1924 in St. Louis.

19. Octavie Pilon-11(Joseph Pilon-10, Angelique Lemay-9, Louise Carrier-8, Andre Carriere-7, Joseph Carrier-6, Charles Joseph Carrier-5, Charles Carrier-4, Charles Carrier-3, Charles Carrier-2, Jean Carrier-1) was born in 1875. He died in 1979. He married Alexandre Parenteau in 1895.

Children of Octavie Pilon and Alexandre Parenteau are:
  i.   Son 1 Pilon.
  ii. Son 2 Pilon.

20. Marie Lamirande-11(Marie Pilon-10, Angelique Lemay-9, Louise Carrier-8, Andre Carriere-7, Joseph Carrier-6, Charles Joseph Carrier-5, Charles Carrier-4, Charles Carrier-3, Charles Carrier-2, Jean Carrier-1) was born in 1858. She married Henri Morand.

Child of Marie Lamirande and Henri Morand is:
  i.   Rosalie Morand, B: 1879.

21. Helene Claire Clarisse Lamirande-11(Marie Pilon-10, Angelique Lemay-9, Louise Carrier-8, Andre Carriere-7, Joseph Carrier-6, Charles Joseph Carrier-5, Charles Carrier-4, Charles Carrier-3, Charles Carrier-2, Jean Carrier-1) was born on 23 Dec 1870 in St. Norbert, MB. She died on 12 Jan 1947. She married Alfred-Boniface Normand on 28 Nov 1893 in St. Norbert, MB. He was born on 09 Nov 1867.

Children of Helene Claire Clarisse Lamirande and Alfred-Boniface Normand are:

	i.	Joseph Albert Normand, B: 1898.
33.	ii.	Alexandre Normand, B: 06 Jun 1904, D: 06 Sep 1973 in Ste. Anne-des-Chenes, MB, M: 05 Apr 1932 in Sandilands, MB.
34.	iii.	Maria Laurencia Normand, B: 22 Jul 1908 in Bedford MB, D: 09 Jan 1997 in Winnipeg MB, M: 16 Oct 1930 in St. Norbert, MB.
34.	iv.	Marie-Cecile Normand.
	v.	Normand.
	vi.	Normand.
	vii.	Elizabeth Normand, M: 27 Nov 1916.

22. Joseph Emery Lamirande-11(Marie Pilon-10, Angelique Lemay-9, Louise Carrier-8, Andre Carriere-7, Joseph Carrier-6, Charles Joseph Carrier-5, Charles Carrier-4, Charles Carrier-3, Charles Carrier-2, Jean Carrier-1) was born on 26 Apr 1880 in St. Norbert, MB. He married Marie Esther Normand. She was born on 09 Sep 1886. She died on 01 Nov 1948 in Winnipeg MB.

Children of Joseph Emery Lamirande and Marie Esther Normand are:

	i.	Esther Lamirande.
36.	ii.	Marie Olivine Lamirande, B: 13 Jun 1909, D: 15 Mar 1999 in Foyer Valade, M: 14 Aug 1928 in St. Norbert, MB.
37.	iii.	Marie Agnes Lamirande, B: 01 Jul 1912, D: 17 Nov 1948 in Winnipeg MB, M: 16 Oct 1930 in St. Norbert, MB.

23. Margurite Lamirande-11(Marie Pilon-10, Angelique Lemay-9, Louise Carrier-8, Andre Carriere-7, Joseph Carrier-6, Charles Joseph Carrier-5, Charles Carrier-4, Charles Carrier-3, Charles Carrier-2, Jean Carrier-1) was born on 05 May 1882. She married Boniface Normand on 11 Apr 1899 in St. Norbert, MB. He was born on 07 Oct 1867.

Children of Margurite Lamirande and Boniface Normand are:
- i. Albert Normand.
- ii. Maxime Normand.
- iii. Elie Normand.
- iv. Philippe Normand.
- v. Adele Normand.
- vi. Elie Normand.
- 37. vii. Marie Rosa Alba Normand, B: 22 Jun 1902 in La Broquerie, MB, D: 1940 in Winnipeg MB, M: 14 Nov 1923 in Batoche, SK.

24. Joseph-Herve Lamirande-11(Marie Pilon-10, Angelique Lemay-9, Louise Carrier-8, Andre Carriere-7, Joseph Carrier-6, Charles Joseph Carrier-5, Charles Carrier-4, Charles Carrier-3, Charles Carrier-2, Jean Carrier-1). He married Josephine Normand.

Child of Joseph-Herve Lamirande and Josephine Normand is:
- i. G. Zephyrin Lamirande, M: 1925.

25. Louis Lamirande-11(Marie Pilon-10, Angelique Lemay-9, Louise Carrier-8, Andre Carriere-7, Joseph Carrier-6, Charles Joseph Carrier-5, Charles Carrier-4, Charles Carrier-3, Charles Carrier-2, Jean Carrier-1). He married Marie Villebrun. She was born on 10 Jun 1859.

Children of Louis Lamirande and Marie Villebrun are:
- i. Celina Lamirande.
- ii. Julienne Lamirande, B: 25 Apr 1884 in St. Norbert, MB.
- iii. Josephine Lamirande, B: 1885.

GENERATION 12

26. Joe Pilon-12(Joseph Pilon-11, Joseph Pilon-10, Angelique Lemay-9, Louise Carrier-8, Andre Carriere-7, Joseph Carrier-6, Charles Joseph Carrier-5, Charles Carrier-4, Charles Carrier-3, Charles Carrier-2, Jean Carrier-1) was born on 05 Jan 1893 in Gabriel's Crossing, SK. He died on 10 Feb 1993. He married Marie Exorine LaPlante on 1914. She was born in 1887. She died on 11 Nov 1970.

Children of Joe Pilon and Marie Exorine LaPlante are:
38.   i.   Lillian Pilon, B: 1929.
39.   ii.   Marie Eileen Pilon, B: 24 Aug 1929 in Rosthern, SK, D: 15 Jul 1989 in Calgary, AB.
40.   iii.   Raymond Pilon.
41.   iv.   Lucien Pilon.

27. William John Pilon-12(Joseph Pilon-11, Joseph Pilon-10, Angelique Lemay-9, Louise Carrier-8, Andre Carriere-7, Joseph Carrier-6, Charles Joseph Carrier-5, Charles Carrier-4, Charles Carrier-3, Charles Carrier-2, Jean Carrier-1) was born in 1898. He died in 1951 when a tractor rolled and pinned him. He married Elmire Marie Fiddler. She was born on 16 Dec 1901 in Fish Creek. She died on 11 Aug 1983 in Rosthern, SK.

Children of William John Pilon and Elmire Marie Fiddler are:
  i.   Emile Pilon, D: 1925.
  ii. Glady Pilon, D: 1925.
  iii. Oscar Pilon, D: 1925.
42. iv. Josie Pilon.
43. v.   Florence Pilon.
  vi. Patrick Pilon.
44. vii. Blanche Pilon.

28. Angeline Georgine Pilon-12(Joseph Pilon-11, Joseph Pilon-10, Angelique Lemay-9, Louise Carrier-8, Andre Carriere-7, Joseph Carrier-6, Charles Joseph Carrier-5, Charles Carrier-4, Charles Carrier-3, Charles Carrier-2, Jean Carrier-1) was born on 08 Dec 1900 in Batoche, SK. She died on 23 Sep 1997 in Regina SK. She married Eugene Leon Guillet on 23 Sep 1920 in Batoche, SK, son of Francois Guillet and Marie Pluchon. He was born on 23 May 1894 in La-Boissarre, France. He died on 05 May 1966 in Prince Albert SK.

Angeline and Eugene

Notes for Eugene Leon Guillet:
Eugene bought a homestead east of Domremy for ten dollars. Shortly after, the First World War began and in 1917, Eugene joined the Armed Forces and was in Halifax ready to go overseas when the news came that the war was ended. Eugene came back home to his farm and built a house and barn. He remained a bachelor for a few more years.

In 1920 Eugene married Angeline (Georgine) Pilon. Angeline had two names. There is an explanation for this. Before her marriage, Georgine

130

worked for Alexis and Georgine Guillet (Eugene's brother) In order to prevent confusion, because the two women had the same name, Alexis nicknamed Georgine (Pilon) Angeline and from then on, that's what the people of Domremy called her.

Children of Angeline Georgine Pilon and Eugene Leon Guillet are:

45.   i.   Agnes Guillet, B: 22 Sep 1921 in Domremy, SK.
46.   ii. Gilbert Guillet, B: 13 Nov 1922 in Domremy, SK, D: 20 Sep 2001 in Domremy, SK, M: 2nd cousins.
47.   iii. Johnny Guillet, B: 08 Aug 1924 in Domremy, SK, D: 07 Jan 2000 in Regina, SK.
48.   iv. Frances Guillet, B: 08 Jan 1926 in Domremy, SK, D: 07 Sep 2003 in Regina SK, M: 21 Sep 1949 in Domremy.
49.   v.   Irene Guillet, B: 12 May 1928 in Domremy, SK, M: 24 Nov 1949 in Domremy, SK.
50.   vi. Leon Guillet, B: 08 May 1930 in Domremy, SK, D: 04 Dec 1999 in Kamloops BC, M: 28 Jul 1949 in Regina, SK.
51.   vii. Aline Guillet, B: 26 Mar 1933 in Domremy, SK, M: 07 Apr 1953.
52.   viii.Raymond Albert Guillet, B: 06 Sep 1936 in Domremy, SK, M: 05 Jan 1957 in Vancouver, BC.
      ix. Paul Ernest Guillet, B: 22 May 1951 in Regina, SK.

Notes for Paul Ernest Guillet:
Natural Mother Aline (Guillet) Lestage. Actually the grandson of Eugene and Angeline Guillet who legally adopted Paul.

For more information on Angeline and Eugene Guillet, see the Guillet Family Tree.

29. Mary Pilon-12(Joseph Pilon-11, Joseph Pilon-10, Angelique Lemay-9, Louise Carrier-8, Andre Carriere-7, Joseph Carrier-6, Charles Joseph Carrier-5, Charles Carrier-4, Charles

Carrier-3, Charles Carrier-2, Jean Carrier-1) was born on 24 Jun 1910 in Batoche, SK. She died on 23 Feb 1981 in Saskatoon, SK. She married Charlie Authier. He was born on 29 Jan 1904 in Valcourt, SK. He died on 18 Apr 1975 in Domremy, SK.

Notes for Charlie Authier:
Charles served in the Air Force from 1941 to 1945. He married Mary in 1945, settled in Domremy, SK where he worked as an electrician until 1967 when they retired to Regina, SK.

Child of Mary Pilon and Charlie Authier is:
    i.   Charlie Emile Authier, D: as an infant.

30. Angelique Pilon-12(Joseph Pilon-11, Joseph Pilon-10, Angelique Lemay-9, Louise Carrier-8, Andre Carriere-7, Joseph Carrier-6, Charles Joseph Carrier-5, Charles Carrier-4, Charles Carrier-3, Charles Carrier-2, Jean Carrier-1) was born in 1903. She died in 1936 at 33 years of TB. She married Antoine Richard, son of Ambroise Richard and Alexina Turcotte. He was born on 12 Nov 1900 in St. Louis, (N.W.T) SK. He died on 03 Jul 1984 in Wakaw, SK.

Children of Angelique Pilon and Antoine Richard are:
53.   i.   Ernest Richard.
54.   ii. Laurent Richard.

31. Blanche Pilon-12(Joseph Pilon-11, Joseph Pilon-10, Angelique Lemay-9, Louise Carrier-8, Andre Carriere-7, Joseph Carrier-6, Charles Joseph Carrier-5, Charles Carrier-4, Charles Carrier-3, Charles Carrier-2, Jean Carrier-1). She married Al Armstrong.

    Children of Blanche Pilon and Al Armstrong are:
      i.   Joanne Armstrong.
      ii. Johnny Armstrong.

32. Alexandre Normand-12(Helene Claire Clarisse Lamirande-11, Marie Pilon-10, Angelique Lemay-9, Louise Carrier-8, Andre Carriere-7, Joseph Carrier-6, Charles Joseph Carrier-5, Charles Carrier-4, Charles Carrier-3, Charles Carrier-2, Jean Carrier-1) was born on 06 Jun 1904. He died on 06 Sep 1973 in Ste. Anne-des-Chenes, MB. He married Valentine Louise Victoria Tourond on 05 Apr 1932 in Sandilands, MB. She was born on 23 Feb 1913 in St. Norbert, MB.

    Children of Alexandre Normand and Valentine Louise Victoria Tourond are:
      i.   Normand.
      ii. Normand.

33. Maria Laurencia Normand-12(Helene Claire Clarisse Lamirande-11, Marie Pilon-10, Angelique Lemay-9, Louise Carrier-8, Andre Carriere-7, Joseph Carrier-6, Charles Joseph Carrier-5, Charles Carrier-4, Charles Carrier-3, Charles Carrier-2, Jean Carrier-1) was born on 22 Jul 1908 in Bedford Manitoba. She died on 09 Jan 1997 in Winnipeg MB. She married Jean-Baptiste St-Germain on 16 Oct 1930 in St. Norbert, MB. He was born on 31 Jul 1899 in St. Norbert, MB.

    Children of Maria Laurencia Normand and Jean-Baptiste St-Germain are:
      i.   Marie-Cecile St-Germain, B: 11 Jul 1931.
      ii.   Marie-Donalda Albertine St-Germain, B: 1932 in St. Norbert, MB.
      iii. Marie-Malvina St-Germain, B: 13 Feb 1934 in St. Norbert, MB.
      iv. Marie-Julliette St-Germain, B: 10 Sep 1935 in St. Vital, MB.

v. St-Germain.
vi. Joseph Alfred Albini St-Germain, B: 16 Jan 1940 in St. Boniface, MB.
vii. Joseph Edouard Denis St-Germain, B: 16 Jan 1940 in St. Boniface, MB.
viii. Jean-Arsene Laurent St-Germain, B: 12 Apr 1941 in St. Boniface, MB.
ix. Victor St-Germain, B: 09 Jul 1952 in St. Boniface, MB.
x. St-Germain.
xi. St-Germain.

34. Marie-Cecile Normand-12(Helene Claire Clarisse Lamirande-11, Marie Pilon-10, Angelique Lemay-9, Louise Carrier-8, Andre Carriere-7, Joseph Carrier-6, Charles Joseph Carrier-5, Charles Carrier-4, Charles Carrier-3, Charles Carrier-2, Jean Carrier-1). She married Rosario Vandal. He was born in 1898.

Child of Marie-Cecile Normand and Rosario Vandal is:
  i. (Girl) Vandal.

35. Marie Olivine Lamirande-12(Joseph Emery Lamirande-11, Marie Pilon-10, Angelique Lemay-9, Louise Carrier-8, Andre Carriere-7, Joseph Carrier-6, Charles Joseph Carrier-5, Charles Carrier-4, Charles Carrier-3, Charles Carrier-2, Jean Carrier-1) was born on 13 Jun 1909. She died on 15 Mar 1999 in Foyer Valade. She married Louis Zephyrin Normand on 14 Aug 1928 in St. Norbert, MB. He was born on 13 Sep 1909. He died on 05 Sep 1951 in St. Vital, MB.

Children of Marie Olivine Lamirande and Louis Zephyrin Normand are:
  i. Rita Normand.
  ii. Martha Normand.
  iii. Lena Normand.
  iv. Andre Normand, B: 23 Nov 1939.

36. Marie Agnes Lamirande-12(Joseph Emery Lamirande-11, Marie Pilon-10, Angelique Lemay-9, Louise Carrier-8, Andre Carriere-7, Joseph Carrier-6, Charles Joseph Carrier-5, Charles Carrier-4, Charles Carrier-3, Charles Carrier-2, Jean Carrier-1) was born on 1 Jul 1912. She died on 17 Nov 1948 in Winnipeg, MB. She married Wilfrid Normand on 16 Oct 1930 in St. Norbert, MB. He was born on 19 Jan 1920 in St. Vital, MB. He died on 4 Apr 1993 in St. James, MB.

Child of Marie Agnes Lamirande and Wilfrid Normand is:
    i.   Emile Normand, B: 1931.

37. Marie Rosa Alba Normand-12(Margurite Lamirande-11, Marie Pilon-10, Angelique Lemay-9, Louise Carrier-8, Andre Carriere-7, Joseph Carrier-6, Charles Joseph Carrier-5, Charles Carrier-4, Charles Carrier-3, Charles Carrier-2, Jean Carrier-1) was born on 22 Jun 1902 in La Broquerie, MB. She died on 1940 in Winnipeg MB. She married Jean Marie Gagnon on 14 Nov 1923 in Batoche. He was born on 28 Aug 1898 in St. Boniface, MB. He died in 1955 in St. Boniface, MB.

Children of Marie Rosa Alba Normand and Jean Marie Gagnon are:
    i.   (Boy) Gagnon.
    ii.   (Girl) Gagnon.

GENERATION 13

38. Lillian Pilon-13(Joe Pilon-12, Joseph Pilon-11, Joseph Pilon-10, Angelique Lemay-9, Louise Carrier-8, Andre Carriere-7, Joseph Carrier-6, Charles Joseph Carrier-5, Charles Carrier-4, Charles Carrier-3, Charles Carrier-2, Jean Carrier-1) was born in 1929. She married George Gervais.

Children of Lillian Pilon and George Gervais are:
  i.   Richard Gervais.
  ii. George Gervais.

Children of Lillian Pilon and Alex Markwart are:
  i.   Wayne Markwart.
  ii. Kelvin Markwart.
  iii. Brenda Markwart.
  iv. Linda Markwart.
  v.   Diane Markwart.

39. Marie Eileen Pilon-13(Joe Pilon-12, Joseph Pilon-11, Joseph Pilon-10, Angelique Lemay-9, Louise Carrier-8, Andre Carriere-7, Joseph Carrier-6, Charles Joseph Carrier-5, Charles Carrier-4, Charles Carrier-3, Charles Carrier-2, Jean Carrier-1) was born on 24 Aug 1929 in Rosthern, SK. She died on 15 Jul 1989 in Calgary, AB. She married Philip Weber. He was born in 1924. He died in 1996.

Children of Marie Eileen Pilon and Philip Weber are:
  i.   Terry Weber.
  ii. Eileen Weber.
  iii. Brenda Weber.
  iv. Brian Weber.
  v.   Denis Weber.
  vi. Raymond Weber.
  vii. Larry Weber.

40. Raymond Pilon-13(Joe Pilon-12, Joseph Pilon-11, Joseph Pilon-10, Angelique Lemay-9, Louise Carrier-8, Andre Carriere-7, Joseph Carrier-6, Charles Joseph Carrier-5, Charles Carrier-4, Charles Carrier-3, Charles Carrier-2, Jean Carrier-1). He married Jane Breland.

    Children of Raymond Pilon and Jane Breland are:
- i.   Eva Pilon.
- ii.   Sandra Pilon.
- iii. Lorrette Pilon.
- iv. Robert Pilon.
- v.   Louis Pilon.
- vi. Derick Pilon.
- vii. Raymond Pilon.
- viii. Kevin Pilon.
- ix. Laurence Pilon.
- 55.   x.   Corrine Pilon, B: 06 Sep 1955, M: 05 Dec 1975.

41. Lucien Pilon-13(Joe Pilon-12, Joseph Pilon-11, Joseph Pilon-10, Angelique Lemay-9, Louise Carrier-8, Andre Carriere-7, Joseph Carrier-6, Charles Joseph Carrier-5, Charles Carrier-4, Charles Carrier-3, Charles Carrier-2, Jean Carrier-1). He married Joan Ford.

    Children of Lucien Pilon and Joan Ford are:
- i.   Ronald Pilon.
- ii.   Sharon Pilon.
- iii. Cheryle Pilon.

42. Josie Pilon-13(William John Pilon-12, Joseph Pilon-11, Joseph Pilon-10, Angelique Lemay-9, Louise Carrier-8, Andre Carriere-7, Joseph Carrier-6, Charles Joseph Carrier-5, Charles Carrier-4, Charles Carrier-3, Charles Carrier-2, Jean Carrier-1). She married Florean Chenier. He died in 1968.

Children of Josie Pilon and Florean Chenier are:
i. Allan Chenier.
ii. Ernest Chenier.
iii. Barbara Chenier.
iv. Aldina Chenier.
v. Patrica Chenier.
vi. Glen Chenier.
vii. Clayton Chenier.
viii. Jenifer Chenier.
ix. Keith Chenier.
x. Lance Chenier.

43. Florence Pilon-13(William John Pilon-12, Joseph Pilon-11, Joseph Pilon-10, Angelique Lemay-9, Louise Carrier-8, Andre Carriere-7, Joseph Carrier-6, Charles Joseph Carrier-5, Charles Carrier-4, Charles Carrier-3, Charles Carrier-2, Jean Carrier-1). She married Reni Pilon.

Children of Florence Pilon and Reni Pilon are:
i. George Pilon.
ii. Marleen Pilon.
iii. Shirley Pilon.

Child of Florence Pilon and Jim Davis is:
i. Diane Davis.

44. Blanche Pilon-13(William John Pilon-12, Joseph Pilon-11, Joseph Pilon-10, Angelique Lemay-9, Louise Carrier-8, Andre Carriere-7, Joseph Carrier-6, Charles Joseph Carrier-5, Charles Carrier-4, Charles Carrier-3, Charles Carrier-2, Jean Carrier-1). She married Al Armstrong.

Children of Blanche Pilon and Al Armstrong are:
  i.   Joanne Armstrong.
  ii. Johnny Armstrong.

Child of Blanche Pilon and Henning Brink is:
  i.   Rebecca Brink.

53. Ernest Richard-13(Angelique Pilon-12, Joseph Pilon-11, Joseph Pilon-10, Angelique Lemay-9, Louise Carrier-8, Andre Carriere-7, Joseph Carrier-6, Charles Joseph Carrier-5, Charles Carrier-4, Charles Carrier-3, Charles Carrier-2, Jean Carrier-1). He married Mary Stocker.

Children of Ernest Richard and Mary Stocker are:
  i.   Ernie Richard.
  ii. Joe Richard.

54. Laurent Richard-13(Angelique Pilon-12, Joseph Pilon-11, Joseph Pilon-10, Angelique Lemay-9, Louise Carrier-8, Andre Carriere-7, Joseph Carrier-6, Charles Joseph Carrier-5, Charles Carrier-4, Charles Carrier-3, Charles Carrier-2, Jean Carrier-1). He married Gertie Caron.

Children of Laurent Richard and Gertie Caron are:
  93. i.   Doreen Richard.
       ii. Reg Richard.
       iii. Karen Richard.

GENERATION 14

55. Corrine Pilon-14(Raymond Pilon-13, Joe Pilon-12, Joseph Pilon-11, Joseph Pilon-10, Angelique Lemay-9, Louise Carrier-8, Andre Carriere-7, Joseph Carrier-6, Charles Joseph Carrier-5, Charles Carrier-4, Charles Carrier-3, Charles Carrier-2, Jean Carrier-1) was born on 06 Sep 1955. She married Marcel Rabut on 05 Dec 1975, son of Joseph Rabut and Florence Joubert. He was born on 02 Apr 1954.

    Children of Corrine Pilon and Marcel Rabut are:
- i.   Angela Rabut, B: 03 Jun 1976.
- ii. Gerald Rabut, B: 25 Sep 1978.
- iii. Geoffrey Rabut, B: 25 Sep 1978.

The Pilon-Carrier Family continues into the Guillet Family Tree.

Ancestry.com, 1901 Census of Canada (Provo, UT, USA: The Generations Network, Inc., 2006), www.ancestry.com, Online publication-Ancestry.com. 1901 Census of Canada [database on-line]. Provo, UT, USA: The Generations Network, Inc., 2006.Original data-Library and Archives Canada. Census of Canada, 1901. Ottawa, Canada: Library and Archives Canada, RG31, T-6428 to T-6556.

Harvest of memories 1889-1995
Domremy History Book

Information written on old pictures

Family submissions